A Member of the Fighting Travers

Major General Sir Robert Travers, KCP, KCMG, KCFM

A MEMBER OF THE FIGHTING TRAVERS

Eaton Davy

BG

The Book Guild Ltd.
Sussex, England

The Book Guild Ltd.
25 High Street,
Lewes, Sussex.

First published 1992
© Eaton Davy 1992
Set in Baskerville
Typesetting by Ashford Setting & Design,
Ashford, Middlesex.
Printed in Great Britain by
Antony Rowe Ltd.,
Chippenham, Wiltshire.

A catalogue record for this book is
available from the British Library

ISBN 0 86332 721 4

LIST OF ILLUSTRATIONS

If neither foes nor loving friends can hurt you,
  If all men count with you, but none too much;
If you can fill the unforgiving minute
  With sixty seconds' worth of distance run,
Yours is the Earth and everything that's in it,
  And — which is more — you'll be a Man, my son!

From *If* by Rudyard Kipling

1

My father was a regular army lieutenant in the Green Howard regiment and was stationed at the regimental depot at Richmond, North Yorkshire when I was born on 1 September 1920. He and my mother first met in County Cork in Ireland when he was acting as ADC to the then Area Commander in 1919. My mother was the only daughter of Brigadier General Joseph Oates Travers, CMG, DSO, who was in command of the Cork Brigade during the Irish troubles at that time, and they were married in Sundays Wells, Cork City on 18 October 1919. My father had been severely wounded during the second battle of the Somme and as a result he was unfit for further active service, hence his appointment to the Staff. A few months after my arrival and early in 1921 my father, realizing that he had little or no future as a regimental officer, resigned his commission. He regretted this decision later on as he received no disability pension as a result of this action whereas those of his contemporaries who stayed on were eventually invalided out of the forces and were granted a disability pension. The family moved to South Devon to a small holding of a few acres near the little village of South Brent, where he hoped and planned to make a living out of pigs and poultry. Many others of his generation ventured their meagre capital in this way and they, like father, came to grief. It was whilst we were in South Devon that my only sister, Eve, was born in Torquay on Christmas Eve, 1924. Fortunately my grandfather was able to bale out the family and we moved once more, this time to Charlton Kings, near Cheltenham. The year was 1925 and I remember the house, called Balcarras, as a big, red brick detached building standing in a large garden with a grass tennis court, at the end of a rough lane which led through fields where grew bluebells in the springtime and mushrooms and blackberries in the late summer months. We employed a cook, a house parlourmaid called Harris and a gardener, and my parents used to give tennis parties with cucumber sandwiches and melon wedges for tea. I remember the melon wedges distinctly because if ever there was any of this succulent fruit left over I was allowed to eat it and the ends of the melon would tickle my ears! It was here in the orchard that I had my first pony-riding lesson. I recall being absolutely terrified and yelling my head off when my instructor made the pony trot and that one 'lesson' was all I had. It put me off ponies and pony-riding for a long, long time!

There was a brick-walled kitchen garden with fruit trees trained up the walls and I remember finding one solitary peach looking ripe and tempting. Imagining that I was Adam in the Garden of Eden I picked and ate it. Delicious! Retribution was nigh, however. A few days later at teatime, my parents were discussing the mysterious disappearance of the peach from the peach tree. I remember flushing to the roots of my hair which, of course, gave them the information they were seeking and I was banished to bed in disgrace!

It was in our first year at Charlton Kings that the General Strike of 1926 took place. My father had joined the Special Constabulary and was often out on duty, usually patrolling the railway line. He also acted as a bus conductor on occasions.

It was at about this time that I became aware of the source of the family finances. My paternal grandfather was joint managing director with his elder brother of the family firm of Arthur Davy & Sons Ltd., Provision Merchants, Manufacturers of Choice Table Delicacies, Café Restaurant Proprietors of Sheffield. My grandfather, being the younger brother, was junior to my great-uncle Arthur who seemed to me to be a very formidable gentleman to whom one only spoke when spoken to. Grandfather on the other hand seemed in my eyes to be a kind and gentle man who made me laugh. To differentiate between my two grandfathers, my father's father was referred to as 'Funny Grandad' whereas my mother's father, the General, was referred to as 'Brent Grandad' for it was at South Brent that I first met him. He often came to stay at Balcarras and he had a large Humber motor car, an open tourer with big, brass headlamps and a hand brake lever outside. He once gave me sixpence for playing *The Bluebells of Scotland* on the piano without making a mistake.

I was sent to Nursery school in Charlton Kings at the age of six years where I learned to read, write and count with coloured sticks. I remember the first day being taken there by my father and rushing down the street after the vanishing car, shouting 'Daddy, Daddy, don't leave me!' Anyway I soon settled happily and remember being able to add, subtract, multiply and divide with the aid of those coloured sticks. I also remember Armistice Day when we pupils had to stand motionless at eleven am on 11 November for the two minutes silence. And what a silence! — everything stopped, and there was not a sound to be heard anywhere! I had just been told about my mother's brother, my Uncle Eaton, who was reported as 'Missing believed killed' at Gallipoli, and the emotional memory remains with me to this day. Uncle Eaton, incidentally, was a very young officer in the Lancashire Fusiliers regiment.

It was at about this time that the military connections of my mother's family were beginning to impinge on my immature mind, and visions of heroism began to form pictorially as I was shown my paternal grandfather's medals.

'One day, my boy, you too will join the army and fight for your king and country.'

Such was the gist of the matter but I was too young to appreciate those prophetic words. My mother was of the 'old school' and was intensely proud of being one of the 'fighting' Travers family. Consequently she was frantically keen on her son growing up to be well-mannered, courteous and considerate — and, of course, of 'officer material'.

It was whilst at Balcarras that I received my first lesson in coping with the unfairness of life. Our next-door neighbour was a Miss Vigors whose front gate opened on to the lane leading past our house and beyond. The lane was unmade and stony, and one day I set off on my fairy cycle to buy sweets at the village shop. In those days it was unheard of to go out without a hat or cap and I had been closely tutored in the courtesy of raising one's cap to a lady of one's acquaintance. Whilst I was not actually acquainted with Miss Vigors I did know her to be a neighbour, and also a friend of my parents.

Imagine my dilemma therefore as I pedalled uncertainly down the lane, avoiding potholes and stones and seeing Miss Vigors coming out of her front gate on foot. I knew that if I extended to her the courtesy of raising my cap I would come to grief off my bike so I decided to take the only other option. I pretended I had not seen her! I pedalled on past Miss Vigors with my eyes fixed straight ahead! That same afternoon I was summoned to my mother's presence and admonished for my failure to raise my cap to Miss Vigors as I had been so often instructed to do. I started to try to explain my predicament but as one did not argue with mother I left the room feeling aggrieved and hard done by.

In order to supplement his income from his small share holding in the family firm and also from a Trust fund set up by the respective families at the time of his marriage, my father had made an arrangement with the manager of the firm's restaurants, Mr Frank Woollen, that he would send in a weekly supply of blackberries and wild mushrooms as they became available, for use in the firm's cafe-restaurants. I can see now, in my mind, a procession of women arriving with chip baskets full of these fruits and fungi. They went round to the stable yard where my father received and weighed these goods and paid the women accordingly. This trade only lasted for about one year as Uncle Arthur, the elder brother, got wind of it and the business was immediately stopped. I will mention here that Uncle Arthur had sired three daughters whereas my grandfather had sired my father who in turn had sired me. Jealousy? Perhaps so, but more of that anon. Whilst on the subject, though, I should mention that my father had endeavoured to gain admittance to the family business by apprenticing himself to a well-known firm of grocers and provision merchants in Piccadilly, London for a year in order to gain a thorough grasp of the trade but Uncle Arthur still refused to have him in the business. He was adamant on the subject. Great aunt Elsie, Uncle Arthur's youngest sister, tried her best to persuade her brother to admit my father into the family firm but Uncle Arthur could not, or would not be moved.

Our stay at Charlton Kings did not last long — presumably the expense of running such an establishment proved too great a strain on the family exchequer so, in late 1927 we moved again this time to a delightful converted mill at Fossebridge which is situated on the Fosse Way between Cirencester and Northleach and which was called The Mill House. This for me was heaven. The River Colne flowed slowly and sleepily past the property at the end of the lawn, and the nursery wing was opposite and detached from the main dwelling house, so my sister and I together with her nanny were away from the parental presence. Eve, by this time, had acquired a taste for riding, having been introduced to that pastime whilst on holiday at Scarborough where there were donkeys on the sands. A Shetland pony named Binker was now on strength and Binker would come into the playroom to receive tit-bits from us at morning break time.

Here I palled up with Frankie Mills, son of the local builder and he it was who taught me to ride my bicycle without holding the handle bars. 'Look, no hands,' he would shout as we hurtled down the country lanes at what seemed like break-neck speed. Of course I had to do likewise. Frankie and I became very firm friends but I was never allowed to invite him into the house for tea, or for any form of socializing. Mother was quite adamant on that point. She said that 'people of our strata do not socialize with trades people'. I was too young to appreciate the double standards involved in this maxim and I continued to grow up with this attitude being drilled into me. Frankie was my friend. We had lots of fun together bird's nesting, stalking our prey and, regretfully, throwing small pebbles at the rumps of a pair of work horses in the field close by and laughing our heads off as they galloped away in sudden fright — farting as they went!

On my return visit to Fossebridge sometime in the 1950s I enquired for Frankie and was very sorry to learn that he had been killed in Burma whilst serving with the RAF during the war.

The River Colne held all sorts of mysteries for me which had to be explored and solved. There were sticklebacks and crayfish to be caught, dragonflies to be followed amongst the kingcups and irises which grew along the river bank and, naturally to a small boy, a raft had to be built to cross the river. There was a wooden foot bridge but a raft would be much more fun, particularly when following footpads or outlaws. The imagination dictated that a raft was essential to the games to be played. This raft, constructed as it was of empty paint tins, a tree trunk and various pieces of drift wood (and anything else that was likely to float!), capsized and sank with all hands soon after launching and so I received my first ducking!

At the southern end of the main house was a tumbledown lean-to shed which my parents converted into a loggia. The shed

11

contained a variety of rubbish amongst which were many pieces of cut and polished marble. What they were doing there I know not — perhaps they were collected by some previous owner for there were many Roman remains in the area, notably the famous Roman villa at Chedworth, some three miles away. My parents acquired two riding horses. Both were chestnut-coloured hunters named Orange Girl and Harkaway, and they occasionally went out with the local hounds. Father also played cricket at Colne St Dennis which was a village some two miles distant. One day he took me with him to a farm sale where he bought two mobile poultry houses on wheels. These were large wire runs with coops at one end and thus he resumed his interest in poultry. He also kept three hives of bees — and I was stung!

2

In the September of 1928, at the age of eight years, I was sent to boarding school at Oakley Hall Preparatory School in Cirencester. The school was run by Major C.F.C. Letts, late of The Rifle Brigade, and his partner Mr Jackson, or Jacko as he was more usually known. These two gentlemen had between them written and published a Latin Primer which I understood was very successful and was used universally throughout the independent preparatory school fraternity. Maybe it still is used but I do not have that information. I was unhappy and miserably insecure at this school from the moment I arrived and in retrospect I do feel that my time at Oakley Hall coloured my outlook and moulded my character to this day for I know myself to be shy and diffident, and inclined to be introspective. I became aware of a mental and physical nervousness which the school failed to help to eradicate. In fact I do feel it made matters worse. I am absolutely convinced that the years between seven and fourteen years of age are the vital ones in the formation of character, emotions and attitudes and, by and large, insufficient thought is given by the majority of parents to the schooling and upbringing of their young. After all, what other 'profession' expects one to be able to cope and to know all the answers without any preliminary training whatsoever. In my own case I felt I was in the way and was consequently dumped away at school just as soon as I reached the age when it was customary for the sons of 'gentle folk' to go away to school. The fact that the headmaster had been a Rifle Brigade Officer of field rank had, I feel sure, helped to convince my mother that this was the ideal place for her son's education. The school's founder and former headmaster, Mr Fosberry, was living in retirement at Fossebridge and I expect he helped persuade my parents to send me to the school which he had founded in Folkestone and moved to its present location.

Admittedly the main school building was large and airy and the grounds were extensive with plenty of room for games and sport. The 'yard' contained a chapel, a large gymnasium with room for a stage at one end, a carpenter's shop and a cottage where Serjeant Major Doubleday and Mrs Doubleday lived. Serjeant Major Doubleday was addressed as Serjeant Major by us boys and he taught us PT, Gym and Boxing and, in the summer term, military arms drill and fieldcraft. The 'arms' consisted of dummy, life size muskets with which we were drilled as if we were professional soldiers. Sometimes the Serjeant Major would creep up behind some unsuspecting boy and substitute a real Lee Enfield service rifle for his comparatively light imitation one, and we would all laugh dutifully at the poor lad's efforts at sloping arms with the unaccustomed weight of a full-sized service rifle. The laughter was always forced as we knew full well that sooner or later one of us would be the victim!

On my very first day at this school and after I had been left there by my parents, I was taken in tow by a group of bigger boys led by one called Mullins who told me to go and hide. I was to be given three minutes before they would come and find me. If I did not hide properly they would 'give me the works.'

I had absolutely no idea of the grounds nor where one could or could not go. The whole place seemed vast, and strange people both boys and their parents, as I now know, seemed to be everywhere. I was panic-stricken and wetted my pants — an unfortunate practice which, together with a tendency to bed wetting, was to dog me throughout my time at Oakley Hall. And anyway, what would 'the works' consist of? This habit of bed wetting would cease in the holidays which suggests to me now that I must have been a bundle of nerves and probably rather difficult to handle. Matters were not made any easier by the rule that anyone who had wetted their bed had to report the fact to the headmaster after breakfast — thus the whole school knew of the fact.

During my time at Oakley Hall there was a boy named Peter Hastings who was my contemporary. He was good at games and became captain of the Rugby XV, the Soccer XI and the Cricket XI, and went on to Stowe School I believe. He subsequently became a successful racehorse trainer. He was the favourite of one of the teaching staff, Mr Knight, of whom I was terrified. Mr Knight was a man of strong likes and dislikes and I obviously fell into the latter category. He seemed to go out of his way to taunt the boys whom he did not like, and I remember once he said to me at the start of an Easter term (the rugger term) that he supposed I would be glad when the term was over as I was a funk on the rugger field. That statement was indeed true but there was no need to rub it in!

I did not care for rugger, and the necessity of hurling oneself at the flashing legs of an opponent who was in all probability bigger and heavier than oneself, and grasping him firmly in a low tackle seemed to me to be asking for trouble and injury! As for falling on the ball and being squashed under the ensuing scrum by a pile of writhing bodies, that gave me a feeling of claustrophobia, and struck me as the height of folly — and still does for that matter! Soccer now; that was different. That was a jolly good game, I thought, and much more scientific and skilful. I received my first XI colours as a goal keeper and did not mind in the least having to receive or try to save a full-blooded shot at goal or even falling on the ball in front of a charging centre forward. In fact I found this to be rather fun, and I much enjoyed the sensation of pitting my wits against my opponent and trying to anticipate his next move. And anyway, there was only one body to cope with and he was not likely to cause me that dreadful feeling of claustrophobia if he should fall on top of me!

I did not make many friends at prep school but a few names come to mind and have remained with me. David Johnstone, the son of a judge and who went on to Fettes school in Scotland was probably my 'best friend'. We both enjoyed reading the exciting stories in *Modern Boy* magazine which was sent to me every week, and we also made up surrealist stories ourselves when we were together on Sunday walks. These Sunday walks were obligatory, in crocodile formation and under the supervision of the duty master. Another friend was John Stott, a somewhat brainy boy who was good at Latin, and who disliked boxing even more than I did! Boxing was, at that time, a compulsory subject and I once had to 'fight' John in the semi-finals of the annual boxing competition. We agreed beforehand that we would not hurt one another! At the end of Round Two of the three round contest, the referee (Major Letts) admonished us both and reminded us that the purpose of a boxing match was to hit ones opponent and thus to score points. So far, neither of us had registered a point on his score sheet! As a consequence and at the first available opportunity, a clinch, we agreed that I was to be the winner. He allowed me to land a few half-hearted punches on his chest and thus gain the contest on points. I was to realize the purpose of his apparent generosity a little later on when I discovered to my horror that I was to meet a boy called Jenner Fust in the final. Jenner Fust was a hard hitter and I was quite sure he would have no such scruples as to who would win our contest! Actually I did win and received a medal for it — a medal well merited and earned, I believe! This just goes to show what can be done when the chips are down! Serjeant Major Doubleday asked me afterwards, as the blood was being wiped from my bleeding nose, 'Why didn't you box like that in the semi-final, Davy?' Needless to say I did not tell him of the pact with John Stott! John went on to take Holy Orders and became Vicar of All Souls Church, Langham Place in London. I am told by one who knew him well that he could have become a bishop but that he preferred to continue his work as a pastor and preacher. Many is the time I have resolved to look him up but, alas, the opportunity has so far not presented itself. I have mentioned earlier that the school had its own chapel so the school had its own choir of some fifteen to eighteen boys of which I was one of that number. Some weeks before the school sports I was picked out to become an alto. Come the following Sports Day, John and I were to sing a duet together. John was the treble and I was the alto and the anthem was John Masefield's poem *Crossing the Bar*. According to my parents our voices blended very well and the duet sounded very nice — praise indeed!

Three of the masters remain in my memory with gratitude and respect. Mr P.M. Garnett was an old boy of Cheltenham College. He took me and two or three others to his old school to attend morning chapel one Sunday. This visit to a public school chapel service broke the ice, so to speak, so that when I eventually went on to public school myself I felt I knew all about attending morning chapel and that it was not all that awesome, thanks to Mr Garnett. He also introduced us to Geometry and was able to explain the mystery of the Pythagoras Theorem, namely that on a right-angled triangle, the square on the hypotenuse is equal to the sum of the squares on the other two sides. He also explained the fact that a recurring number (which was quite dotty anyway!) would go on and on to the gas works and even beyond. We could see the gas works in the far distance and it did indeed seem a long, long way!

Yes, learning was fun with Mr Garnett. I believe he eventually entered the Royal Navy which was a great loss to the teaching profession as he was most certainly a boy's man.

Mr Bickersteth came from Westmoreland and was a keen ornithologist and naturalist. He it was who taught us boys, amongst other things, how to catch, ring and release birds without hurting them or damaging their feathers, how to prepare and keep a bird watcher's notebook, not to rob bird's nests, not to keep wild birds in cramped cages but to give them room to fly and exercise their wings, and all kinds of interesting and exciting facts concerning wild life generally. 'Look and listen' was his catchphrase. To him I shall always be grateful for instilling in me my abiding interest in all things to do with nature. He, too, was a boy's man.

Mr Woolward, a rather elderly man, introduced me to the French language and, so far as I was concerned at any rate, he must have made a good job of it for that tongue has remained a favourite of mine to this day, and I used to teach it myself many years later with some degree of success. I believe I modelled my teaching of French on Mr Woolward. He drove a Talbot Tourer 'Occasional Four' motor car and came to the school part time to teach. To our great regret he retired soon afterwards and his Talbot Sports tourer was no longer parked in our line of vision. However, Jacko had an Alvis Speed 20. Now that was a car and no mistake! Its speedometer dial went up to ninety miles per hour and when he was asked by some precocious boy whether he had ever driven his car that fast, he would just smile and say: 'Wouldn't you like to know!' This answer only served to enhance the mystery and romance and we were all convinced that Jacko must have reached at least a hundred miles per hour! He got married during my time at Oakley Hall and we were given a half-holiday to mark the occasion. Hurrah for Jacko! Would we be given a half-holiday for each ensuing little Jackos? I never knew the answer to that question for up to the day I left the school there was no such luck!

Sports Day was one of the highlights of the school year. The

17

paddock being the nearest games field to the school was marked out for the occasion and all sorts of equipment and farm implements were stationed at suitable intervals around the perimeter of the field for the Obstacle Race. Included amongst the obstacles was a large tarpaulin sheet secured to the ground by pegs and the competitors had to crawl underneath this sheet. Apparently one year I arrived at the tarpaulin at the same time as another lad and, '*toujours la politesse*', I let the other boy through first. My parents ragged me about this show of 'politeness' on my part and even recalled the incident some years later. This rankled with me as it seemed to contradict their maxim of consideration, courtesy and service to others, which dicta were constantly being drilled into me. They and in particular my mother were determined that their son would grow up to be considered as a polite, nicely-mannered and well brought up young man, but this attitude did not encourage me to be competitive.

One of my friends at school introduced me to guinea pigs as pets. I thought they were fascinating creatures and longed to have one as a pet. Antony Waite had invited me out one Sunday during the summer term. They lived in the country near Stroud in Gloucestershire and not only did they have ponies to ride but they also had guinea pigs — hundreds of them, or so it seemed! I was so captivated by these delightful animals that I wrote home and obtained permission from my parents and gave Antony an order for a breeding pair to be sent to me by train early on in the following summer holidays. I forget the price charged but they duly arrived and we collected Cherry and Othello from Totnes Railway Station. These two guinea pigs were to form the foundation of many, many guinea pigs; my father said that it was the best thing he ever did to give permission for me to breed guinea pigs as it taught both me and my sister the 'facts of life' such as could never be done by word of mouth alone! My guinea pigs were housed in a chicken coop enclosed in a wire run but they soon 'outgrew' this restricted area and were allowed to run free in the long grass by the side of the driveway and in no time at all we could muster forty-eight both young and old. They did a stalwart job in keeping the grass down, and thrived in their freedom. They must have saved father a fortune in petrol through their grass control!

On the other side of the valley lived Mrs Goldsmith. Mrs

Goldsmith kept horses though I never saw her mounted on one of her steeds. She employed a groom by the name of Buckingham who was a frequent passer-by when he went out exercising the horses. Mrs Goldsmith was an ardent supporter of the RSPCA amongst other good works. One day during my absence at school, she came to tea with my parents, accompanied by her two terriers. The terriers were left outside during her visit and when the time came for her departure it was discovered that her dogs had slaughtered *all* my guinea pigs. Forty-eight little bodies were found lying around in the grass by my parents. Never a word of apology, or regret, from Mrs Goldsmith.

Another form of home discipline comes to mind and that involved not speaking unless spoken to. I well remember daring to offer my opinion on Neville Chamberlain's mission to Munich when he tried to appease Adolph Hitler and thus to stop any further territorial claims in Europe. At this time I was seventeen years of age and my mother turned to me and said:

'When we want your opinion we shall ask for it. Meanwhile, don't interrupt, it's very rude.'

Little incidents such as these caused me to retire into my shell and thus not enter into any discussion or argument. One thing my mother in particular did achieve was to ensure that her son did not become a politician! It all depends, of course, on the temperament of the child as to whether the parents should encourage or discourage him or her to speak their mind. A proper balance is very difficult to achieve and this is one more example of the difficulties facing parenthood, and the need for training in the task. My late wife and I have two children and I can only hope that we did a better job on our two sons than my parents did on me.

Later on a further maxim became the norm when my father told me in all seriousness: 'We Davys are not Pot Hunters.' This must have been our Quaker ancestry coming out! All these 'messages' coupled with the somewhat overbearing authority of prep school life together with the domineering presence of my mother during school holidays made me a diffident and retiring child and certainly not one to throw my weight about nor to make my presence felt. I was, however, led to believe that my parents were responsible for the removal of Mr Knight from the school teaching staff, so I must have told them of my fear of that gentleman. However, whenever I broached with them the subject of competition I was told that if I were good enough I would succeed or be selected for the team. Personally, and with the benefit of hindsight, I do not think that that was very good advice as it tended to make me sit back and not really try. 'The Lord will Provide' or 'The State will Provide' syndromes. After all, where the majority of young people are concerned, the carrot is an incentive and the blissful joy of achievement can be most rewarding.

Major Letts seemed, again with hindsight, to be over-fond of administering corporal punishment either with the cane, or with a clothes brush on a bare backside. The administration of a caning took place at the foot of a bed in one of the dormitories so, if the instructions were to proceed to number three dormitory, you knew you were for the cane. Clothes brushing however took place in the passage leading to the said dormitory so you were, at least, forewarned as to which of these two alternatives you were in for. I received many such chastisements during my time at preparatory school, some for failing to report my bed-wetting. These 'accidents' had to be reported to the headmaster after breakfast so the whole school would see that you were on the mat. Bed wetting would stop during the holidays which seems significant. Another punishable 'offence' was to collect two or more black lines on consecutive weeks for poor work in any particular subject. These marks were read out to the whole school on Saturday mornings and the rewards ranged from a full red line under one's name for very good or outstanding work through to half red or dotted red and black lines to full black lines. Woe betide the boy who had a full black line beneath his name! For a nervous and highly strung child these weekly sessions in front of the whole school were purgatory especially when you were told to 'Go upstairs and wait.' I wonder what would happen today? Such physical assaults on a defenceless person would not be tolerated and I am sure the authorities would issue a summons if such 'brutalities' ever came to their notice. It was not done to 'make a fuss' about such things so I do not suppose 'they' would ever hear about it!

I was bitten by the cricket 'bug' at the age of eight and a half years when Serjeant Major who took the junior game sent me up to the colts after two or three games. Thenceforth I was hooked! I loved cricket and still do, and can vividly remember watching an inter-school first XI match from the boundary in the year 1930 when I was not quite ten years old. A boy named Cazenove was bowling for the school at the time and I vowed to myself that I too would be out there playing for the school. I did just that and was awarded my first XI colours but I cannot remember when or why. I do, however, remember being awarded my second XI colours. The match was being played against Glengarth school on a sloping pitch in the paddock. I discovered that if I could pitch the ball on or about the leg stump, then the slope would turn it into a leg break. I believe I collected five wickets that day, thanks to the lie of the land, and was hailed as a future prodigy! When faced with the plumb first game pitch, things were not so easy but I did learn something about flight and cutters, and the cover drive, all of which stood me in good stead later on.

My paternal grandfather, or 'Funny Grandad' of whom I was particularly fond, lived in a seemingly large house near the top of Manchester Road in Sheffield called West Royd. The extensive gardens sloped away from the house to a dell at the bottom which served as a Pitch and Put Course and which also accommodated a cricket net. Many were the happy hours spent down there when grandfather would bowl his leg breaks at me. His gardener, Wormald by name, who lived in the lodge at the entrance to West Royd, would be drafted in from his horticultural duties in the garden. Wormald was a left arm bowler of some considerable skill and cunning and had, in his younger days, been a stalwart member of the Hallamshire Cricket Club — one of the oldest clubs in the country of which my grandfather subsequently became the president.

When we went to stay with grandfather in the summer months we met the Pringle family. Dr Pringle was the local doctor in a working class district in the east of Sheffield and the family consisted of two girls, Margaret and Kathleen, and a boy named George. George was also keen on cricket so he and I would disappear down to the dell for some practice, leaving his two sisters, my sister and grandfather's daughter by his second marriage, Muriel by name, to their girlish games.

One summer's morning we all went to Bramall Lane cricket ground to watch a county match. Yorkshire was playing Nottinghamshire and I remember that match very clearly because Yorkshire, under the able captaincy of Brian Sellars, won the toss and had decided to bat first. Grandfather was on

21

the Yorkshire county committee and subsequently became the county president so we all enjoyed preferential treatment with seats in the directors' stand and luncheon in the dining room. To revert to the match: my hero, Herbert Sutcliffe, was out, caught in the gully off Voce for a very low score. The next morning came a telephone call for me from grandfather suggesting that I should go straight down to Bramall Lane where he would meet me. Down I went to the county ground and I was taken to the practice area. There, to my astonishment and surprise, was my hero, Herbert Sutcliffe, batting in the nets whilst three of the Yorkshire team's fast bowlers were bowling at him, amongst them was Bill Bowes. They were under the direction of Brian Sellars and were bowling at a great pace, pitching the ball just short of a length outside the off stump. This was a salutary lesson to me — it did not matter in those days if your opening batsman was also the opening batsman for England. As a batsman one did not get caught in the gully off a short ball outside the off stump. One either got on top of it and hit it for four runs — or else one left it alone and let it pass harmlessly by. Ah, yes! Those were the days! Brian Sellars was a great captain, respected by his team and well able to hold his own amongst many famous names in the Yorkshire XI — Bowes, Sutcliffe, Leyland, Verity, Wood. The list seems endless, I can smell the smell of cigar smoke to this day and my mind will shoot back to Bramall Lane whenever that familiar odour of cigar smoke comes my way!

We often saw the Lascelles brothers there. They kept themselves very much to themselves and did not mix with the 'hoi polloi!' How I revelled in those visits to the county ground where I could rub shoulders with my idols of the cricket field.

3

On another occasion I was taken by grandfather to the team's dressing room to be introduced to the Yorkshire team. My grandfather at that time was on the county committee so he was quite well known amongst the players. Maurice Leyland had dropped a catch that morning whilst fielding at deep extra cover. As I was introduced to the players we came to Leyland, and I well remember my grandfather's comment after introducing his grandson, as well as Leyland's reply.

'Now then, Maurice, you should have caught that catch. It was a sitter.'

'Aye, I knows that, Mr Davy,' came the reply, 'but we don't drop 'em on purpose, tha' knows.'

Grandfather was a pretty good bowler and was able to drop the ball on a good length with consummate ease. This practice against his accurate bowling was to stand me in good stead later, for he was invited to play in the end of term parents match against the school XI in 1934 and caused havoc amongst us young batsmen. I remember the conference between him and the wicket keeper, Mr Rosser, before he bowled his next over. This resulted in the school batsman being stumped whilst well out of his crease. To everyone's astonishment and disbelief the boy was given 'NOT OUT' by the square leg umpire. That batsman went on to make a respectable score! At the end of the over I heard the umpire (the headmaster, in fact) say to my grandfather:

'I'm sorry I could not give the batsman out, Mr Davy — your wicket keeper MUST let the ball pass the stumps before whipping off the bails!' A salutary lesson to all concerned and I can see grandad now, his fingers to his mouth, saying to himself, 'Well, upon my word!' No recriminations, no anger, no argument even though his cunning plan had misfired! I believe this was and still is the only occasion on which three generations had taken part in a parent's match and, alas, I cannot recall the result — but I still have a photograph of 'We Three'.

Towards the end of my time at Oakley Hall I, together with the other leavers, were given a Sex Lecture by the headmaster. I found this subject painfully embarrassing and can recall little about it except thinking at the time that the whole business of Intercourse and Procreation of the human species must be rather messy and disgusting! Looking back from the distance of time it must have been extremely embarrassing for the headmaster too!

In July 1934 came the end of the summer term and also the end of my stay at Oakley Hall Preparatory School. I had passed the Common Entrance examination to Malvern College and so left my prep school with few regrets. There were, of course, moments of happiness and fulfilment but on the whole and with the benefit of hindsight I found that the school gave me little encouragement and it was largely responsible for my shyness and sense of inadequacy which handicaps have dogged me throughout my adult life. I have learned to rise above these self-doubts when faced with a challenge but I am quite sure that my preparatory school days coupled with the lack of demonstrative affection from my mother have undoubtedly coloured my attitude towards people and situations and left me with a feeling of insecurity and, try as I may, I cannot recall ever being hugged or cuddled by my mother though I must not create an impression that she did not love me. That would be quite wrong — she was a woman of strong will and was always the dominant figure in the family — impetuous and outspoken on occasions and very conscious of her breeding as one of the Travers family who could trace their lineage back to The Conqueror. I am quite sure she loved both my sister and me equally but was incapable of being demonstrative in this regard. I was reminded constantly of this side of my ancestry during my childhood and I can only suppose that this was part of her plan to instil in me, her only son, a pride in my forbears and an ambition to enter the armed forces of the Realm and thus carry on her family tradition.

I was christened at the age of six weeks and given the names of Arthur Eaton. Arthur is, by tradition, the forename of the eldest or only son in the Davy family and Eaton is likewise the forename of the eldest son in the Travers family. Permission had to be obtained, of course, from the 'head of the family' to enable this name to be given to me as I was not in fact a Travers.

During my prep school days the name of Travers was added and became my third forename by dint of use, though it does not appear on my birth certificate. It has consequently been a nuisance and is often queried by the Powers That Be, notably Insurance companies and the like. The idea was that I should eventually have the name added by Deed Poll, probably as a part of my surname and with a hyphen i.e. Travers-Davy, but I found the unofficial addition to be troublesome enough without the addition of any further complications. Anyway I was quite content to be just Davy without any embellishments, no matter what were mother's views.

In 1930 the family moved yet again, this time back to South Devon. There were two intermediate rented homes, one at Babbacombe and another at the village of Barton before we finally settled into Winsland, near Totnes. Winsland was a super house and home — an old farmhouse in the middle of about twenty acres and situated some one and a half miles from Totnes off the old Plymouth road, and the family was to remain there until driven out by an enemy bombing raid in 1941. The main railway from Paddington to Penzance ran past the property (there was one field between the house and the line) and here my sister and I could run free and the only restrictions on our activities were those imposed on us by Eve's governess, Miss Fribbance, commonly referred to in the family as 'Fribby'. Miss Fribbance, as I remember, was a bit of a martinette and I bitterly resented being under her control when home for the school holidays.

After all, I was now ten years old and had long since left the age of being ordered about by nannies and governesses! I did run into real trouble on one particular occasion and received 'six of the best' from my father who was far from being a violent man. I bear him no grudge for the beating which was both merited and well worthwhile! Eve detested porridge but was made to eat it. When I came home for the holidays I had to take my breakfast in the school room where Miss Fribbance reigned supreme. Having got rid of 'Fribby' on some pretext or other I unscrewed the seat of the piano stool and poured the remains of Eve's porridge into the resultant aperture. This ruse was fine and Eve received due praise for eating up her porridge 'like a good little girl'. Came the moment of truth though when Miss Fribbance had cause to lower the seat of the piano stool to suit herself. After a few turns the end of the screw-head met the 'mess of porridge' in the body of the stool. As the screw-head was turned further into the body of the cavity so the porridge oozed out until finally the grizzly truth was revealed. Miss Fribbance was furious and I had to own up. My dastardly deed was duly reported to my father who was compelled to administer the inevitable punishment, not very hard though, and in a little while he complimented me on my initiative. Miss Fribbance left us soon afterwards and Eve went off to boarding school in Swanage.

One of our more fool-hardy games was a form of Wells Fargo. There was a super orchard on the property, full of mature cider and other breeds of apple trees. These made ideal places from which to drop onto unsuspecting riders who happened to be passing beneath. Our long-suffering ponies must have wondered what on earth was happening when suddenly the one or other of us would land on its back without any warning, and emitting blood-curdling shrieks at the same time. The pony would then be urged into a gallop as we two riders would pretend to be pursued by 'baddies' and had to reach the base to warn of impending danger from redskins or outlaws. These games became rather too lifelike when we decided to instil a little realism into the proceedings. I possessed a Diana Air Pistol and I regret to say that the occasional lead pellet would strike the pony on the rump and send it off at break neck speed, usually with my sister on board! Looking back now I realize that I was very fortunate in having a sister, although four years younger than me, who would enter wholeheartedly into those boyish games. Leading on from these Wells Fargo style games was a further enterprise which entailed harnessing the pony to an old sledge. This, of course, opened up all sorts of possibilities — the pony and sledge became a stage coach and one of us would be the highwayman and either hold up the Stage or pursue it at full gallop in and out amongst the trees. It was better still when one of us was aboard the sledge as then it was less likely to turn over. When we found an old pram it was better still as the pram

26

had wheels and thus less effort was required by the pony. 'Harness' had to be manufactured, by pleating straw for a collar and covering this with any old cloth used as discarded vests or other articles of personal clothing.

One of the problems consequent upon our move down south was the travelling to school at the commencement of term, for the journey entailed changing trains and stations at Cheltenham, for the train from the south west arrived at Cheltenham Spa whereas the train for Cirencester left from Cheltenham Malvern Road. The problem was solved by my being put in the charge of the guard as far as Cheltenham where Serjeant Major would meet me and arrange for a town porter to transfer my trunk and tuck box to Malvern Road Station to catch the Cirencester train.

During one of my off-spells at school when nothing seemed to go right and my work had consequently deteriorated, I received a letter from my father in which he threatened to remove me from Oakley Hall if my work did not improve and to send me to the local grammar school in Totnes. At that time I was growing up with the notion that only tradespeople's sons and those sons of 'lesser' mortals went to grammar schools, so this threat had the desired effect. I have often wondered what the result would have been had I had the 'guts' to call my father's bluff, just for the hell of it! As a matter of fact the local King Edward VI Grammar School had a very good name academically and many of my 'illicit' friends were pupils at that school so I would probably have been quite happy and have done quite well there. This could never have happened, of course, as my parents would have lost face in the district. And so, eventually, came the day when I finally left my Preparatory School for good to start the next chapter of my life.

At the top of the field fronting the house ran the main road to Plymouth. The field sloped upwards from the house to the road, and along the stretch of road was a thorn hedge in the midst of which grew a gnarled ash tree. This tree was hollow and also had a sort of platform some ten feet from the ground formed by the boughs which grew therefrom. This tree was an obvious choice for a tree house. With a small amount of judicious spade work an entry could be gained into the hollow trunk of the tree so that one could, quite literally, disappear at a moment's notice. It was quite dry and cosy inside, and as far as we knew, only Eve and I were aware of the existence of our hide out. The platform outside formed an ideal start for a tree house and it was not long before we had rigged up some walls from old sacks, and we were thus able to remain there unobserved by the outside world. Many were the pranks we played on an unsuspecting public including, I regret to say, spraying our quarry with water from two stirrup pumps which we had acquired from a source unknown. The highlight of this comparatively harmless prank was when a small touring car went past with its hood down. It was a cloudy day and, just as the car went past us, we sprayed it with water from our stirrup pumps. The car stopped, the occupants got out and proceeded to raise the hood. Oh, what rapture! Oh, what bliss! We had succeeded in fooling them!

At the end of my last term my father came to fetch me in the car together with the trailer. On our way home to Totnes we were to spend the night at the Queens Hotel in Burnham-on-Sea North Somerset. We had spent many a family holiday there and knew the Batemans, who were the owners of the hotel, quite well. My parents were also well acquainted with other people round and about.

Not far from our destination and where the main road was fairly wide and straight we were going along at about thirty-five miles per hour when there was a loud ringing sound behind us. Father had been 'gonged' by the police for exceeding the speed limit with a trailer. He had been exceeding thirty miles per hour and received a summons! The case duly came to court and he was fined ten shillings. The year was 1934.

4

During the final two years of my time at Oakley Hall there had been numerous discussions as to where I should go after leaving preparatory school. These discussions were between my mother and father, as I was present with a listening brief only and was not asked for my opinion or preference. Naturally I hoped to be sent to Malvern College because my father had been there himself just before World War One. Major Letts, on the other hand, was all for Haileybury, he being an Old Haileyburian. My father stuck to his guns and insisted on my going to his old school which he had left in 1913 to go to Sandhurst and thence to the war. I was thus duly entered for his old house, Number Three, whither I was delivered by him in September 1934. There were eight of us new boys that term and we were all entertained to tea by the housemaster and his wife, the Reverend, and Mrs W.O. Cosgrove. I had met Mr Cosgrove once before when he came to Oakley Hall to vet me. He had been the housemaster of Number Three for about a year and was also the college chaplain. He was known to us boys as The Dean. He and Mrs Cosgrove had three daughters who were nicknamed by my father as Jack, Fred and Peter, after the names of their dog, their house porter and their rabbit respectively. Father was always finding nicknames for people and he also created his own vocabulary such as 'dycles' for cold, 'tat tah' for walk etc. This was the start of five happy years to be concluded in July 1939.

The college with its extensive grounds is situated on the western outskirts of the town of Great Malvern in Worcestershire and it nestles beneath the towering heights of the Malvern Beacon, part of the Malvern Hills of which Sir Edward Elgar was so very fond. The pupils were accommodated in ten separate houses which are grouped mainly around the perimeter of the

29

grounds, each house being self-contained with private quarters for the housemaster and his family, and dormitories and studies for the boys. Each house had about fifty boys at that time so that at full strength the school roll numbered about five hundred pupils. There was intense rivalry between the different houses, and house patriotism was encouraged and fostered by the housemasters and boys alike. Housemasters would go out on 'recruiting drives' to various preparatory schools and I imagine that sporting and/or games ability played a big part in the selection process, especially in those pre-war days. I know I came to Number Three house with the reputation of being a useful boxer, cricketer and footballer but I regret to say I was to let down the house over boxing.

One of the first hurdles to be overcome after entering college life was the Prefects' exam. This ordeal happened at the end of the first three weeks after which time one was supposed to have learned the names of all the other housemasters, the head boy's name of each house, the different house colours, the nicknames of different masters and so on, in fact, everything to do with the college including everyday slang. To achieve fluency in this department, two yearling fags were allocated to our studies to coach us in these mysteries, and woe betide them if their pupils did not come up to scratch!

I soon settled into the routine of college life and set about trying to make good. Fagging was quite good fun, I thought, and we 'new bugs' were quick off the mark when the cry of 'FAG' rang out from one of the prefects. The last person to arrive at the source of the call had to do the job which could be anything from cleaning shoes, brushing coats, making toast at the prefects' room gas fire (this only happened on Saturdays and Sundays and a piece could be made for oneself), as well as going to the Tuck Shop (Keep the change) or delivering a message to a 'pre' in another house, usually about games or something similar. The world of college was large and formidable after preparatory school and the customs and traditions seemed strange and somewhat pointless at first. Some boys had one hand in their trouser pocket and others strolled about with both hands in their pockets; we new boys were not allowed to put our hands in our pockets at all. Some boys wore rounded collars whilst other bigger boys wore pointed collars. The permutations of colours on the peaked caps seemed endless whilst some bigger boys sported umbrellas and others had silver-nobbed canes. These latter were school prefects and we youngsters treated them most deferentially, almost to the point of raising our caps to them. One lad in our group did just that and was hauled over the coals in front of the head of house at assembly time.

All prefects had the power of administering corporal punishment with the housemaster's permission which was usually given if just cause could be proved, so the wretched culprit would be told to wait in his study after prayers, until called down by the junior prefect. Whilst I myself did not receive a prefects' beating, many of my contemporaries did, and I considered it then and I still do consider it to be both degrading and obscene to the giver and futile to the receiver because it goes contrary to all human instincts. It is unsporting, inhuman and obscene to inflict pain or physical punishment on a defenceless animal (including human ones). It is uncivilized to expect the recipient of physical violence to remain still while being subjected to the often vicious blows of his fellow human beings, and not to defend himself against attack which would, after all, be his natural reaction. I am quite well aware that this is a debatable point and one is often led to wonder whether or not the muggers and other cowardly bullies of our society would not be better citizens if they were chastised for their crimes against the elderly and weaker members of our society. I am certainly not advocating an 'eye for an eye' philosophy but I am just wondering. The Isle of Man used to administer the birch to their offenders and the crime rate was virtually nil. Since the Common Market legislation took a hand the birch, whilst not abandoned by statute, is not used today and the crime rate seems to have risen dramatically. Quite recently a member of the island constabulary was stabbed whilst on duty. There is surely a lesson for us here somewhere?

Early on in our college careers we new boys were ordered to the house changing room one evening to be vetted by the prefect of games as to our respective potential as boxers. Apparently the idea was to field a boxing team to try to capture the inter-house boxing cup. It appeared that my 'fame' as a boxer and medal winner at prep school had preceded me for I was immediately told to put on some gloves and spar with one of the prefects. This was a command one ignored or disobeyed at one's peril so I had a go. Superior height, reach and strength were too much for me and I was left in no doubt at all as to who was the boss. Exhausted, deflated and smarting from some nasty blows to the face, I was 'taken down a peg or two' and I discovered afterwards that it was assumed that because I was a medal winner at prep school I must be a swank and therefore I must be taught a lesson. I was yet to learn about boxing weights but the psychological damage was done and I vowed I would never box again — which vow I have so far managed to keep! When the college boxing competitions took place I was, most fortunately and genuinely, laid up with influenza and could not compete but I accepted graciously the commiserations of my housemaster!

As time went on I became more and more integrated into college life and soon found myself caught up in the many and varied extra-mural activities on offer to the college pupils. I much enjoyed music and singing and I became a member of the college choir but not until after my voice broke in 1935. Then I became one of the basses and joined the Choral Society. There was carpentry and woodwork on offer so I took that as an extra as well as Art under an elderly Old Malverian named Mr Gilmore, or Gilley as he was called by us boys. It was not long before I sat for and passed the Oxford and Cambridge School Certificate with a mere two credits (or honours as they are now called) in English and French, and all this time there was talk at home of my going to Sandhurst and making the army my career. Here I must acknowledge a debt to my prep school because the set Shakespearean play for the School Certificate for that year was *The Tempest* (or was it *Twelfth Night*?), both of which I knew almost by heart as I had had a part in both of them when the school put on its annual play.

One Tuesday morning during the early part of the summer term I received my usual weekly letter from my mother in which she accused me of taking a bottle of 'Camp' coffee from the kitchen cupboard at home. She went on to say that if I wanted something like that I had only to ask for it, but to take it without reference to anyone was 'tantamount to stealing.' I had certainly not taken the bottle of coffee, in fact I disliked Camp coffee and was very hurt by this unjust accusation. In my reply I denied vehemently having stolen anything from the kitchen cupboard and certainly would not have taken a bottle of Camp coffee. No further reference was made to this incident for a week or two and then came a cryptic sentence in her weekly letter which ran as follows:

'I have spoken to cook about the Camp coffee. She told me she has used it all and didn't expect me to take the matter up with you.'

There was no word of apology at all.

My friend Laugharne Richardson who used to come with his parents when they parked their caravan in the orchard, taught me how to make gun powder. Laugharne was a scholar at Cheltenham College and was one year older than me and had started studying science.

I had been out shooting a few days before his arrival and had collected some half dozen expended cartridges during the day. I immediately went into Totnes to acquire the necessary ingredients and started at Boots The Chemist where I asked for some saltpetre. I then went to another chemist for some sulphur and some charcoal which three ingredients made up the gunpowder mixture. Laugharne also taught me how to make up a delayed action fuse by soaking a length of string in a solution of the saltpetre. Having packed tightly an empty cartridge case with the well mixed gunpowder, we inserted the dried fuse, lit it and stood well back and under cover. The ensuing explosion could probably be heard for miles around. Our cook, Grace, was just in the act of putting the joint of roast lamb into the oven when the big bang went off. The joint landed on the floor and lunch was half an hour late that day whilst cook was busily engaged in retrieving the meat which had slithered across the linoleum covered floor of the kitchen and had finished up behind the sink unit.

My father, unknown to us, was in the lavatory at this time. When it came round to our Saturday 'dose' of Syrup of Figs, he declined to accept his turn. He reckoned that the effects of an unexpected explosion not far from the lavatory window was much more effective than any number of teaspoons of Syrup of Figs and the effects of that experience would do him for the following week! Father could see the funny side of this episode and tried for all he was worth not to let mother down but he could not restrain himself when it came to the Saturday dose!

It was now September 1936 when I moved on to the Army Vth where I came up against such subjects as Statics and Dynamics which I was quite unable to comprehend, and anyway

Sports, Games and Choral Singing were much more interesting and satisfying. It was at about this time that I received my one and only caning from my housemaster. During a Geography lesson my neighbour made me a bet that I could not flick some ink and hit a factory chimney on a large photographic poster on the wall some six feet away. To this day I cannot imagine why I fell for it but try I did and the resultant wet ink was found by the geography master, Mr Bolam, after our departure to another lesson. The class was subsequently summoned to return and I had to confess to being the guilty party. On another occasion I incurred The Dean's displeasure when he discovered me with a crystal radio set in my bed after lights out. One of our group was a radio 'buff' and had made a crystal set which worked. I am always fascinated by gadgets and he told me how to make such a set for myself and also where to purchase the necessary parts. I duly acquired the equipment, built my set and took it to bed with me. I dropped a long length of wire out of the window to act as the aerial and the earth wire was attached to the central heating pipe which ran right around the dormitory cubicles. I had just tuned in to Jack Jackson and his Savoy Orpheans when I spotted The Dean's flashlight reflected on the ceiling. The Dean was doing his rounds — and he *would* choose tonight! It was too late to dismantle everything so I feigned sleep, hoping that my open window and the aerial wire would not be noticed. The Dean saw the open window and came into my cubicle to close it, and this was the moment when he saw the aerial wire. He roused me from my 'slumbers' and told me to bring the crystal to him the next day. Now, I reasoned that a crystal bears a striking resemblance to a small piece of coke so I selected a suitable piece of coke from the boiler room and presented myself to The Dean's study at the appointed hour and handed over the piece of coke which I had selected very carefully to masquerade as my crystal. He accepted the coke and I went away well pleased with my little deception after he had told me to collect it from him at the end of term. When I went to collect my 'crystal' from him at the end of term as instructed, he handed it over and said, without any expression on his face:

'Here you are, Davy. I don't know how you managed to get any reception with this.'

I am quite sure he 'rumbled' my ruse but was too much of

a sport to tell me!

Only once more did I incur The Dean's wrath and that was over a matter of a rubber stamp. I had found a very old, dust encrusted rubber stamp at the back of a cupboard in the house library and, being curious as to its purpose, I cleaned it, 'hawed' on it and pressed it firmly on to a corner of the wall where I reckoned it would not be noticed and where it left the required information in very faint blue lettering: No 3 House Library. My curiosity satisfied I thought nothing more about it until many days later the head prefect announced that The Dean wished to see the boy who had disfigured the wall in the house library by imprinting a rubber stamp thereon. I presented myself for interview, prepared for the wrath to come, and was given a good telling off. I recall one sentence of this wigging and am constantly reminded of it to this day. 'It displays the same mentality as that of people who write lewd remarks on public lavatory walls.' If I had had need of a cure that did it, and whenever I have cause to use a public convenience I am invariably reminded of the 'meat' of The Dean's message which I did feel at the time to be rather unjustified and also inappropriate but I can appreciate the purpose of it. Would that others had learned and taken to heart the same lesson!

By the time September 1938 had arrived I was already a house prefect and unsuccessfully passed the previous summer term as captain of the house cricket XI. Our house had been knocked out of the inter-house cricket competition in the first round, thanks largely to my own ineptitude and inexperience as captain. I had also sat for the Army examination which I failed miserably — my heart was not in it and I was quite literally drifting with the current; the current being my parent's preconceived plan that I was going into the army. For my own part I was enjoying life at college which I treated as a glorified sports club and had no thought for the morrow as to what it would bring or what I was going to do for a living. Looking back now, I suppose the main influence on this negative attitude of mine was the fact that my father did not have a regular job though he was a Special Constable and did go to the office occasionally. I do not suppose I ever really thought about what I was going to do — and was saved in this dilemma by the declaration of war against Germany.

During the course of the summer holidays of 1938 I joined

the Devon Dumplings Cricket Club — much to my mother's delight. Her own father, my 'Brent Grandad' had been a member when he was a young officer in the Devonshire Regiment whose regimental depot was in Exeter. I recall one of my best bowling performances during this time. The summer of 1938 was a particularly wet one. I was one of the Dumplings team to play against a London touring team called Chiswick Park, at Newton Abbot. The visitors must have won the toss and decided to bat first. During the course of their innings I was given the ball and managed to take seven of their wickets for a total of twenty-two runs. Unfortunately rain prevented any play on the following day so the match was inconclusive. Little did I know that I was to meet up with one of the opposing players some years later when I started work in Sheffield after the war.

During the course of the Christmas term 1938 I was made a College prefect and, come the Easter term 1939 I did achieve another minor ambition and was appointed Head of House for my remaining two terms.

War clouds were gathering in Europe and we young men were beginning to wonder which of the armed services we should grace with our presence. We began to plan our part in what looked like the inevitability of hostilities. I got stuck into my studies for a change and worked many a long evening after the remainder of the house had gone to bed, trying to master the perpetual mysteries of Statics and Dynamics, Chemistry and Physics. When the re-sit came I did quite well but not well enough to pass into Sandhurst. I did in fact work it out at the time that if I had achieved the same marks the previous year as I had gained on the re-sit exam I would have passed into Sandhurst quite high up, such was the demand for places at that time.

Another diversion was the possibility of gaining my first XI colours at cricket. I began the term with no great ambition of getting into the college team though I did have a tenuous hope of getting into the college second XI — but this hope was purely a matter of speculation. The master in charge of cricket, Mr Staniforth, had noticed that I was a potential or natural in-swing bowler, though I had not discovered this talent for myself. He devoted a great deal of time and effort into developing my delivery, and he was instrumental in creating in me a tactical approach to the game. My initial inclusion in the first XI was against the Worcestershire County Colts team on the county ground at Worcester where I succeeded in capturing three of the opposition wickets with comparatively slow deliveries. As a result of this achievement I was awarded my XL cap and I began to have ambitions of greater things. The next match was a home game against Cheltenham College when again I was fairly successful with slightly faster in-swing deliveries, though I had not yet learned to vary my pace or method of delivery. After that match I was awarded my XXII cap. Things were going nicely but that was as far as I was to climb. A match against an M.C.C. team proved disastrous and then came the army examination which coincided with the annual contest against Repton school. I missed that match as I had to go up to London for interview and thus failed in my new-found ambition to gain a first XI colour for cricket. I failed the army exam too and was thus in disgrace at home.

On my departure at the end of the summer term 1939, The Dean presented me with a copy of Rudyard Kipling's poems, a beautifully bound volume printed on rice paper, in which he had written 'In grateful recognition of two good terms' and signed 'W.O.C.' I shall always treasure that book and its inscription for I held my housemaster in very high regard.

Towards the end of my last term at Malvern College I, together with another young man called Dodds, was invited to join the Devon County cricket team for their two two-day matches against Oxfordshire and Dorset, so off we went to Oxford where we presented ourselves at the Mitre Hotel where the Devon team was staying. It was a very wet summer and I believe the Oxford match was inconclusive. I do remember being called upon to open the bowling and being thrashed all over the field. Two overs were enough to convince our captain, Ronnie Seldon, that I was not on form so I was taken off and not invited to bowl again either in that match or against Dorset at Sherborne.

When the results of the army exam were published in the daily papers the family went through the list with a 'fine tooth comb,' but my name was not amongst them. The atmosphere was highly charged. I, on whom such high hopes had been pinned, had let them down. I had failed.

'After all we have done for you and the sacrifices we have

made for you, you have failed.'

I was saved by Adolph Hitler! War with Germany was declared on 3 September 1939. It was a Sunday. We were all having our 'elevenses' in the conservatory and I was re-arranging the moss and rocks in my vivarium at the time — the salamander had nowhere to hide and I felt for it. I wished most earnestly that I had somewhere to hide as well! Then the idea came to me — I would go away and stay with my friends the Colmans whose daughter, Dorothy, ran a riding stables at Churston Ferrers. Thither I departed and stayed for two weeks until the clouds of disappointment had blown away at home.

On 7 October of that fateful year I drove to Exeter and presented myself as a volunteer for His Majesty's forces. I applied for a commission in the Royal Artillery, was put through the medical exam, given a half-crown and told to go home and await my call-up. I have often wondered what prompted me to apply for the Gunners and have come to the conclusion that it must have been a sort of back-handed swipe at my mother — I had failed to get into Sandhurst but nevertheless I would get a commission in the Royal Artillery instead!

5

I joined the LDV or Local Defence Volunteers, soon to be renamed the Home Guard, under the command of Captain Niles, the proprietor of the Seven Stars Garage on The Plains at Totnes. Our weekly parade took place on The Plains and we were given various duties of a military nature to perform. My platoon was responsible for patrolling the stretch of railway line between Totnes and Newton Abbot and we were issued with an assortment of weapons. Those who possessed or had access to a shot gun brought their own firearm but they had to supply their own ammunition. There were no rifles to start with so a number of men carried pitchforks or other suitable weapons; one I remember had a bill hook stuck in his belt which he explained to us left his hands free to grapple with an enemy adversary! The day came when we were issued with a Hotchkiss Machine Gun. This weapon was a first world war veteran and it was loaded by means of a flexible belt into which the ammunition was inserted. We had no ammunition for it but the effect on morale was enormous! As I was the youngest and, thus presumably the fittest, I was given the doubtful privilege of being Number One on the Machine gun. I lugged this weapon around and pretended to load, aim and fire. No instruction manual came with the gun and, as no one had had any experience with it, I and my Number Two had to find out by trial and error how it worked, how to strip down and re-assemble it, load, aim and fire it. What fun it all was, and how seriously we performed our duties!

By the time the month of December arrived I was becoming restless and, like so many of my generation, anxious to get into uniform and be away to the war. Much correspondence with the appropriate department at the War Office indicated that 'they' could manage without my services for a good while yet and so I applied for and got a job as an assistant master at Winchester Lodge Preparatory School for Boys in Torquay, to start the following January 1940. The interview was interesting. On presenting myself for interview one afternoon I was met by the headmaster, Mr George Butler, who put me at ease straight away for he was a keen cricketer and was, in fact, captain of Torquay Cricket Club. The memory of an incident during the course of that interview has remained with me. The Butlers had two children a daughter named Josephine of about nine years of age and a small son, Jeremy, of about two and a half years old. After tea the entire family excused themselves on some pretext or other, leaving me alone with the small son. I remember getting down on my hands and knees and playing with young Jeremy on the floor. The game consisted of pushing a 'dinky toy' to and fro to each other which gave Jeremy huge delight with much childish mirth on his part and shrieks of forced enthusiasm on mine! We were caught red-handed by Mr and Mrs Butler and the result was that I was given the job. I wonder if I was classified as 'good with children?' Their daughter, Josephine, became an air hostess with BOAC and was killed in an air crash at Singapore in, I believe, 1947.

My salary at Winchester Lodge Preparatory School was to be £35.00 per term or £105.00 per annum. To present-day minds this will probably seem derisory but, out of my first term's salary of £35.00 I was able to purchase my very first motor car — a 1929 Austin Seven Saloon. This car had belonged to a naval officer who had driven it all the way down from Scotland on his posting to his ship at Devonport. It had a fabric body which was torn in two places and which I repaired with some oiled silk bought for the purpose from a local chemist. This I glued over the tears and subsequently painted in black paint bought from Woolworths. The car also sported a brass (golden) eagle in its radiator cap. The purchase of my first car was four pounds and ten shillings (£4.50) and the Third Party Insurance was a further ten shillings — total outlay £5.00! My parents had accumulated a stock of petrol amounting to fifty gallons in a drum and I regret to confess that I soon made a considerable inroad into this store!

When I joined the Home Guard (Dad's Army) I palled up with one of the mechanics at the garage from whence I bought the car, and he made me a thin brass gasket to replace the correct one. We were thus able to increase considerably the compression ratio and the car made a roaring sound rather reminiscent of a sports car. The only drawback was that the engine was inclined to overheat. One day I was on my way to play cricket in Torquay and was ascending the long hill from Totnes when there was a violent eruption. Clouds of steam and water gushed forth from the radiator as the golden eagle took flight. The bird flew away under the force of the pressure generated in the radiator and vanished from sight. Whither it flew I know not but it took to the wing never to be seen again by me and I was compelled to insert an ordinary nut and bolt in place of that golden eagle. I swear to this day that that car was never the same again!

My time at Winchester Lodge was both rewarding and interesting. The teaching staff had been seriously depleted through calls to the Colours so I was the youngest member. There were about thirty boarders and the same number of day boys and I was put in charge of Form III as their form master — a class of some fourteen pupils who started by testing me out. I was fortunate enough to be able to put a stop to any nonsense of that kind as I was not long out of school myself and was wise to the wiles of the young.

I like to think that we were all great friends and I used to enter into their games during break time. The summer term was the best though. The other members of staff were generally elderly and were prepared to do weekend duty, thus leaving the way clear for me to go off to play cricket. For this reason I rarely did a weekend duty at all and was free to play cricket for Torquay most Saturdays. This was indeed a bonus and when I was invited to turn out with a scratch County team against a scratch RAF team at the Recreation Ground at Torquay I was in seventh heaven. The RAF team included such names as W.R. Hammond (captain), Bill Edrich, Maurice Tate, Leslie Ames, George Macaulay and the presence of such well-known performers caused a deal of local interest. When the appointed day arrived the ground was rapidly filled with some three thousand spectators who were asked to subscribe a small entrance fee which went towards Red Cross funds. The RAF won the toss and elected to bat. Bill Edrich was one of the openers and soon his partner was out. In came Wally Hammond, the man whom 3,000 spectators had come to watch. The atmosphere was

41

electric. The master craftsman was about to perform. Almost immediately the famous cover drives were in evidence and the runs were coming along at a fast rate. I was fielding at extra-cover when a full-blooded Hammond drive came scorching across the turf in my direction. I have always enjoyed fielding and, running in as usual, I picked up the ball and threw it accurately to the batsman's end. Our wicket keeper received the ball cleanly, whipped off the bails with a cry of: 'How's that?' The great Wally Hammond who was still some two or three feet outside the crease was well and truly out. The groans of the crowd could be clearly heard for they had come to see the master and I had run him out. I wished the ground would open up and swallow me but I was soon to be mollified by a typical sportsman's gesture. When we went in to lunch, Wally Hammond was waiting on the pavilion steps. He picked me out of the fielding side, and patted me on the shoulder with a word of congratulation on a fine piece of fielding. I cannot remember much about the remainder of the match except that I did score four runs, I believe, off the exceedingly fast bowling of Bill Edrich. I wish I could say that those four runs were from a boundary off a classic shot but no, what happened is not really clear in my mind. The ball clipped the shoulder of my bat, flew over the heads of the two slip fieldsmen and ran to the boundary. Not to worry, four runs is four runs and they all look the same in the score book! I was out soon after — bowled neck and crop, and I must in all truth confess that I did not really see the ball at all!

I was able to enjoy some lovely games of cricket with Torquay, the Devon Dumplings and Devon County teams during the summer of 1940 but all good things do come to an end and early in December I was off to the war. After several letters to the War Office the Powers That Be wrote to say that they required volunteers to go to India with a view to taking commissions in the Indian Army. This would involve attending a six month course at the Officers' Training School at Bangalore in Mysore and would I be prepared to go out there. If so, we would all go out as cadets and would be paid as for the rate due to a serjeant in the British Service until we received our commissions. I accepted and was eventually summoned to Aldershot just before Christmas in preparation for shipment to India. Thus began the next part of my life, as a member of His Majesty's forces.

6

Willems Barracks, Aldershot which was to be my home for some four weeks before embarkation, had been condemned in the 1930s as unfit but they were apparently good enough to house us cadets. My father who was by this time happily back in uniform as a Group Officer in the Observer Corps was wearing RAF blue with black rank badges. He was responsible for the setting up of a string of observer posts throughout the South West area. He gave me a few words of advice before I left for Aldershot amongst which was the golden rule that in the army one should never, but never, volunteer for anything. Unfortunately I was to ignore this sound advice when we were due to go out on a field training exercise. The platoon serjeant entered the barrack room and barked: 'Anyone 'ere ride an 'orse?' A momentary flash of memory crossed my mind when I recalled the college O.T.C. Field Days when one or two of the boys were called upon to act as the General's gallopers. This was, presumably, the same thing I thought and so, utterly heedless of paternal advice, I said:

'Yes, serjeant.'

'Good man,' he replied. 'Coal fatigue for you. Report to the quartermaster's stores immediately.'

Ah, well, it could have been worse. At least I was spared running around the countryside. The coal was delivered by horse and cart and the job was done and finished by four thirty pm. It was nevertheless a perfect reminder not to volunteer for anything in the army!

One Sunday morning the company was marched down to the garrison church for morning service. Standing just inside the porch was the company serjeant major whose job it was to see that all ranks were decently and correctly turned out. As we

43

approached the door we removed our head dresses and then the serjeant major's voice rang out:

'Take yer bloody 'at orf in the 'ouse o' Gawd, yer ruddy 'eathen.'

One of our number had forgotten to remove his cap!

Early in January 1941 we of the advance guard entrained for Glasgow and the train stopped at Sheffield Midland station on the way. The sight of Sheffield, although it was quite dark outside, brought back memories of happier times and I could but wonder whether and when I would see the place again. On arrival at Glasgow some time the next morning we were marched to our quarters and found ourselves billeted in a disused factory just outside Gourock — a dilapidated building infested with vermin. Route marches were commonplace and on one occasion we were fallen out for a twenty minute break. Three of us entered a co-operative store in search of some refreshment. We were befriended by a middle-aged woman who insisted that we return with her to her flat for a cup of tea. We climbed an iron staircase outside a tenement building and entered a dingy apartment which was her home. It had a curtained-off alcove at one side from whence came sounds of continual coughing.

'My daughter,' she informed us. 'She's not been at all well.'

The daughter certainly did not sound too good at all, and I suspect that the poor girl was suffering from TB but one did not like to interfere, apart from saying that we supposed the doctor had seen her. Tea in enamel mugs, and meat pies were put before us and we had to pretend to enjoy our meal. All the time there was the sound of that distressing cough coming from behind the curtain. We soon excused ourselves as we had to report back on parade and we left this kind and generous woman who called to us from the stairs of her apartment:

'Good luck to you, lads, and take care of yourselves.'

We were just in time to rejoin the march back to our billets.

Having stowed the baggage on board the M.V. *Highland Chieftain*, the main body of the draft arrived and we all embarked on this converted meat ship. Before the outbreak of war she used to ply between the Argentinian port of Buenos Aires and Liverpool bringing Argentine beef to England in her refrigerated holds. These holds had been converted now into troop decks and we were packed into them like sardines in a barrel. Much was the grumbling to be heard and there was nearly a mutiny until the Officer in Charge took a hand in sorting things out. Whilst wandering round the decks I met an old school friend, Desmond Manners, who told me that there would be a call for volunteers for the anti-aircraft section the next day and he strongly advised me to be one of the volunteers. I told him about the incident back at Willems Barracks and also about my father's advice against volunteering for anything but he assured me that this was a genuine piece of information. The 'carrot' was that the AA section was housed on their own in the fo'c'sle and that it had bunks to sleep on. This was surely better than the troop deck floor or table-top — but, what was it father had said: 'Take a tip from me, my boy, and never volunteer for anything.' I had already been caught out once — was it worth the risk of being caught out again? This matter had best be investigated so I visited the fo'c'sle and there were indeed spring bunks. A member of the crew assured me that the AA section was to be billeted there so I reckoned the risk was worth taking. The next day whilst we were still at anchor we were called on parade and our company officer duly called out: 'Will all those men who have had any experience with a machine gun take one pace forward.'

Well, I mused, I did handle a Hotchkiss in the Home Guard. I know I had not fired it but he didn't say that, did he? I took the required pace forward and so found myself number one on the Lewis Gun on the starboard side of the bridge. 'Oh, my God, what had I let myself in for?' Not only was it a Lewis Gun which I had never even handled before, let alone know how to load and fire it, but the position was enough to turn anyone's stomach! The port and starboard bridge platforms were built out from the superstructure so that the platform itself was suspended over the water. My number two had not even handled a machine gun — but he had seen one in a military museum and had heard about the spring bunks!

Our prowess, or lack of ability as machine gunners was not put to the test fortunately and the convoy steamed undisturbed to Freetown by way of Iceland and Newfoundland. This extended route was done purposely to avoid enemy aircraft and submarines. Winter storms were frequently encountered and the seas were often mountainous. Being on duty on any of the machine gun positions was no sinecure but those of us on the port or starboard gun positions were often in no condition to take on an enemy aircraft should one be encountered. A few days out from port it was considered very unlikely that enemy aircraft would bother us so the AA guns were 'stood down' until the convoy came within range of the Vichy French and German bases in Africa. We dropped anchor off Freetown and remained there for a day or two in the sweltering humid atmosphere of the bay. No one was allowed ashore. Soon we were off again, this time bound for Cape Town and thence to Durban where we were to change ships from the M.V. *Highland Chieftain* to the M.V. *Windsor Castle*.

On the voyage, the day came for our inoculations. All members of HM Forces had to have anti-tetanus, typhoid and cholera inoculations which were recorded in our pay books (AB64s), so we were lined up in single file to receive our injection against typhoid fever. There was no question of changing the needle of the syringe — it felt blunt enough when the AA platoon was injected so I wonder what it must have felt like to the last one of the several hundred 'passengers!'

As we advanced pace by pace for our turn, the man in front of me keeled over and collapsed in a dead faint at my feet. Immediately the man behind me did the same thing and I was left standing between the two prostrate bodies!

Some hours later the effects of the typhoid shot became apparent and I together with several others retired to our bunks feeling very feverish and ill. These effects lasted for about twenty-four hours.

On arrival at Durban we were allowed shore leave so, in company with a friend, I set off on foot for the city where we both hoped to find a Turkish bath and a barber after which we felt we would be in a position to enjoy the luxuries of civilization once again. As we walked along the harbour front ruminating on the joys of life to come, a large car pulled up alongside us and the driver enquired if we would like a lift. Naturally we accepted and after eliciting the information that we were looking for a bath and shave, the driver who introduced himself as Mr Van Ampstel, took us to a public bath house where we could get a Turkish bath to remove the rigours of our confinement in the troopship, and he also pointed out a good barber's shop where he said he would pick us up at an appointed hour and take us to his home for an evening's relaxation. He was as good as his word and, at the appointed hour, he arrived to collect us.

His home was beautiful and set in well laid-out gardens on the outskirts of Durban, a part of a prosperous suburb of the city. Mrs Van Ampstel had obviously been warned of our coming, for a gorgeous high tea was laid on for our enjoyment — they were truly delightful people who seemingly could not do enough for us. They took us under their wing, entertained us to the cinema and on to a gracious cocktail party given by the French consul. During our last evening ashore the Van Ampstels took us to an elegant sea front hotel for dinner and there they obtained from us our home addresses so that 'we can write and tell your folks at home that we have seen you and that you are OK.' They proved not only true to their word but they also sent food parcels of all sorts of goodies which were unobtainable at home — dried fruits, nuts, tea, coffee, and so on. Alas, later on I heard from home that Mr Van Ampstel had been posted to Borneo by his company and had been subsequently captured there and shot by the Japanese. Mrs Van Ampstel had escaped with her children back to South Africa and had written this news to my parents.

We reached Bombay in early March 1941 having been nearly nine weeks en route and were soon on a train for the two-day journey to Bangalore. It was very hot and airless on the train and we took turns to stand in the open doorway of the carriages so that the passing air would cool our bodies which were unaccustomed to the heat. On arrival at the Officers' Training School we cadets were allocated our quarters after being divided into companies. I was in number eight Training Company, and each of our quarters housed two cadets and there was an Indian servant, or bearer, to look after two rooms. The bearer was responsible for getting us up in the mornings, keeping our kits and clothing clean and smart, and doing other odd jobs for us as the need arose. This was to be our home for the next six months, and so my room mate, Derek Gerhold, and I set about learning how to become good officers in the Indian Army.

7

We officer cadets were soon taken in hand by the staff and made to 'jump to it, sir'. The member of staff appointed to instruct us in weapon training and fieldcraft was a certain C.S.M. Workman whose home town was Sheffield. It was not long before he found out my connection with that city so I was henceforth known as 'Townee'. Another remarkable coincidence was that the OTS Quartermaster was a Lieutenant Colonel Newton who had started his working life as a junior employee in our family firm before deciding on an army career. 'Tis a small world indeed!

The first day or two was spent in finding our way around, drawing kit, bicycles etc and we soon discovered that we were to be treated very much like overgrown schoolboys, with strict rules and regulations to be observed. For instance, it was forbidden for any cadet to drive a motor car or to ride a motor bicycle; the British United Services Club was out of bounds, as were certain parts of the town bazaar. The reason for these irksome restrictions was that the previous draft of cadets to pass through the OTS, Bangalore, were tea planters from Assam and they had caused some disturbance amongst the local populace. We were to pay the penalty for their misdemeanours.

The six month course passed very quickly but not without some hiccoughs to myself. I had become acquainted with the ADC to the Area Commander. The said ADC kept a few horses which I was invited to ride whenever I felt inclined. This was fine until I discovered there was a price to be paid for the privilege. Contact was immediately broken off. The same man invited me to bring a friend out one Sunday and he would take us out in his car to Mysore, about forty to fifty miles away, to see the gardens and other sights including the Maharajah's palace and gardens. This was a lovely trip and we passed any number of places of historical interest connected with General Wellesley's campaigns. During lunch, however, our host became somewhat inebriated; in fact he was paralytic and quite unable to drive his car, a Buick Straight 8. We had to be back by six pm that evening as there was a night training exercise to attend so it was imperative that we return in time for the parade. My companion could not drive so between us we bundled our host onto the back seat, I took the wheel and off we set on the return journey to Bangalore. We deposited our 'host' at his bungalow, collected his driver to take us back to 'barracks' and thought no more about it.

We cadets would be appointed to various 'commands' each week and it was my turn to be Cadet Company Commander. On the Tuesday morning I marched my company to the Mess hall for breakfast, where stood the school commandant, Brigadier Gilbert, watching the parade. Nothing unusual in that so I marched up to him, gave him my smartest salute and asked his permission to dismiss the company to breakfast. Permission was granted and the troops dismissed to breakfast. Unknown to me, however, I had been recognized as the cadet whom he had seen driving a car the previous Sunday. I was summoned to the company office and marched in: left-right-left-right-halt-cap off. There behind his desk sat Captain John Stone, Seventh Gurkha Rifles, our Staff Company Commander. Details of my 'crime' were read out and I was asked if I had anything to say. There was plenty I could say but I replied in the negative and was then asked if I knew the rule forbidding cadets to drive a car. I agreed I did know the rule and I was asked again if I had anything to say. I declined to say anything and was 'sentenced' to ten days C.B. (Confined to Barracks) which meant that I could not leave the precincts of the school other than on official duty. Black Mark Davy!

On another occasion I received a mosquito bite on my right index finger which went septic and the poison ran up my arm creating a rash, until it reached a gland under my right arm pit. I was quite unable to use the arm, let alone give a salute, and was hospitalized after the Medical Officer had had the finger dressed with sulphonamide powder to no avail. I was in considerable pain and running a temperature but even the hospital doctor did nothing except prescribe dressings on the finger, including sulphonamide powder. In desperation I called the ward sister and asked her for a hot water bottle to put under my armpit. She demured, saying the doctor would not permit it but after his departure she brought me the 'hottie' which I placed against the swollen gland under my armpit. The effect was almost immediate and after two days all traces of the swelling and infection had disappeared. On being discharged from hospital I met the sister just coming on duty and I was able to thank her for 'smuggling' the hot water bottle to me. I remember her reply:

'You are a very lucky young man. You could easily have lost that arm.'

At 'half term' in June we were all given seven days leave. In company with Antony Morris I went to Ootacamund which is a hill station situated in the heart of the Nilgiri Hills and where the 'sahibs' and their 'memsahibs' from Madras would go during the hot weather. A rack and pinion railway wound its laborious way up and around the hills until Ooty was reached, 7,000 feet above sea level. The cool air was glorious and such a contrast to the humid air down below on the plains where the monsoon weather was beginning to gather, for the monsoon was soon to break. We enjoyed the freedom from military discipline, we played tennis, walked the hills and went on a game-watching trek through the jungle on an elephant. We did not see much game apart from some sambre and spotted deer but our elephant did put his foot in it. He trod on a hornet's nest, and immediately a swarm of very irate insects were all around us. Antony and I jumped down and ran for safety whilst the mahout and elephant made off at a lumbering trot leaving us to face the wild beasts alone and unarmed! Order was soon restored and we climbed back on board to complete our trek without further mishap! The week's leave soon passed and we were back again at school to face the second half of the course. We learned a number of quite useless drill movements, especially those concerning a parade with bicycles. On those rare occasions when the company had to parade with bicycles the whole company would line up in two ranks with their bikes. The commands would then be issued: 'Move to the right (or left) in column of half sections. Half sections — right' whereupon all front wheels were turned in the appropriate direction. 'Quick march' would then follow, whereupon the squad would set off, pairing up in twos. 'Prepare to mount,' the left foot is placed upon the bicycle pedal whilst the right foot executes a variety of jig until relieved by the command: 'Mount' when all troops would sling their right leg over the saddle, and order was restored once more. What fun it was, as Cadet Company Commander, to delay that command to mount!

About half way through the second half of the course we were invited to express our preferences for posting, the preferences to be detailed in order of preference. Naturally I put down the 4th P.W.O. Gurkha Rifles as my first choice as I had family associations with that regiment. A great uncle, Lieutenant Colonel Robert Travers, known in the family as Gurkha Bob, had commanded their first battalion in France during World War One. I was lucky in being posted to the Regimental Centre in Bakloh and I discovered later that 'Gurkha Bob' had written to the Commandant of the Regimental Centre on my behalf. Another of our cadet company, Paul Messenger, was also posted there so we set off together on our posting leave to Bombay from whence we planned to take the Frontier Mail train to Amritsar and then on by local train to the rail head at Pathankot. The train journey was uneventful and on arrival at Pathankot we were told that the civilian bus which we had to catch, would be leaving in about an hour's time; a curry lunch was therefore taken in the refreshment room on Pathankot railway station.

The bus was an ancient Bedford, driven by an equally elderly Sikh. We 'sahibs' were given the front seats on the bus whilst the remaining passengers all piled in as best they could with their goods and chattels. Most passengers gained a seat inside the bus but those who were unsuccessful had to sit on top thus raising considerably the centre of gravity of the vehicle! The chattels consisted of an extraordinary variety of possessions such as boxes, cases, live chickens and even a goat or two! We drove through the town at break neck speed, scattering people, poultry, dogs and tonga ponies in all directions until finally we reached open country, and the turn off for Dalhousie and Bakloh. As the bus climbed the tortuous road the air became thinner and the driver apparently more light-headed, sped round blind corners with the blast on the horn. In fact he seemed to drive with one hand permanently pressing on the horn button. We paused for breath and refreshment at a Dak bungalow and finally arrived at Tuna Hatti, the turn off for Bakloh, where a military

51

truck driven by a Gurkha from the regimental centre was awaiting our arrival. At last we had arrived. We reported to the adjutant who was expecting us, escorted to the quartermaster who was responsible for allocating quarters, and I was allotted number nineteen bungalow. There I found a servant, or bearer, named Moladad Khan awaiting me and an officer from our second battalion, 'Slogger' Martin, already in residence. 'Slogger' was an ex-guardsman and was awaiting drafting to the second battalion in the Middle East. We were to become good companions throughout the next few months.

8

One of the first actions to be performed by a newly-joined officer was to call on the senior officers of the station so I dutifully did the rounds of the relevant bungalows, leaving my recently acquired 'Visiting Cards', engraved of course with my name and the full regimental title thereon. It should be remembered that at this time in September 1941, the Japanese armies had all but reached the Burma-India border, things were not going well with the allied forces. Never mind, the British Raj must appear untroubled!

As a newly joined officer I was 'dined in' to the Officers' Mess as the guest of Major Hubert Madge on 24 September 1941. This was a great occasion in the life of a young officer. The night was set aside as a Regimental Guest Night when all single officers in the station who were members of the Mess would attend. It was a formal occasion when the rules of etiquette were strictly observed. As guests, both Paul Messenger and I were technically in command — no one could leave the table or leave the Mess until we had withdrawn but we did not play any pranks that night. We were far too overawed!

We newly commissioned officers were not much use to the regiment until we had acquired a rudimentary knowledge of the native language Urdu, as well as an understanding and knowledge of the men we were to command — their names and regimental numbers, their castes, their homeland and its topography and so on. In order to remedy this deficiency and accelerate our integration into the military machine a Young Officers' Course was devised under the direction of Captain Robert Williams, a regular officer who was one of the last cadets to pass through the Royal Military College, Sandhurst. He was awaiting a posting to our second battalion. We were put through our paces after attending morning parade with our companies and we acquired a reasonable prowess in unarmed combat, bayonet drill and the like as well as regular sessions with the Munshi or teacher, in order to polish up our Urdu in which we were to be examined later on. A pass in Urdu carried a fixed reward of One Hundred Rupees, a tidy sum of money in those days.

Sometime in October came the Hindu festival of Dushera which can be likened in name only to the Christian festival of Harvest Thanksgiving. The festival entailed a day's holiday culminating in the slaughter of a variety of animals ranging from chickens and ducks to a full grown bullock or steer. As far as I can remember the Regimental Havildar (Serjeant) Major had the honour of wielding the sacrificial kukri and the future of the unit or regiment was in his hands. The head of the bullock *must* be severed from the body with *one* blow of the kukri. If this were accomplished all would be well.

A post was firmly affixed into the ground and the animals were tied to this post by their horns in order of magnitude, starting with the smallest, and thus presenting the executioner with a clean target, this being the neck. As can be imagined, this was a bloody business indeed and the ground soon ran red with blood. First the chicken — off with its head. This was easy and a murmur of approval ran round the assembled spectators who were seated in tiers around and about, forming an amphitheatre. The body of the chicken ran off before collapsing in a jerking heap. Various other animals suffered the same fate until the moment for which all had been waiting — the sacrifice of the bullock. A deathly hush descended on the assembled company as the bullock was dragged reluctantly to the post and secured by a rope around its horns. The RHM approached with the sacrificial kukri which he placed on the animal's neck on the precise spot on which he had decided the blow should fall. As he raised the two-handed kukri above his head one could feel the drama rising to a climax. Down came the blade and with one clean blow the head of the bullock was cut from its body which fell to the ground. A roar of delighted approval rose from the spectators as they clapped each other on the back: all would be well for the ensuing year; the crops would grow; the harvest would be good; the regiment would distinguish itself and all would be well with the world. Meanwhile the corpse was dragged away to be given to the 'Untouchables', and then the dancing began.

We young officers who were witnessing this gory orgy for the first time, were looked after by a Gurkha Officer from our company. They plied us with 'raksi' which is a potent form of rum (closely related to methylated spirits, I thought!) and we became more and more inebriated as the evening wore on. Some of us attempted to join in the dancing and at some time well after midnight I felt it was time to go. Now I discovered the true meaning of that well-worn phrase: 'The spirit is willing but the flesh is weak'. I was assisted to my bungalow by (so I am told) Subedar Birman and laid on my bed. The next morning my bearer, Moladad Khan, brought me a mug of hot, sweet tea; my head throbbed, my eyes were bloodshot and I was expected on parade at seven thirty am. Thanks to my bearer, some Alka Seltzers and a cold bath I 'made it' on time, correctly dressed in well creased shorts, a clean crisp shirt and polished, shiny boots. As I arrived on parade ahead of my company commander I was met by the company Subedar, Subedar Birman. He approached me smartly, gave his usual crisp salute which I acknowledged, and then reported the parade state. I noticed there was not a flicker of a smile on his open face and, having completed his part, he saluted again, turned about smartly and returned to his place in front of the company. I have absolutely no idea what he told me but I would have to give the same report to Captain Williams when he appeared on parade. I hoped that possibly he would not 'make it' but my fervent prayer was not answered. Captain Williams appeared just as the quarter guard bell sounded seven thirty hours. I brought the company to attention and reported to the company commander a jumble of manufactured figures. He accepted my report with no apparent disbelief and then bade the senior Gurkha officer to carry on with the parade. Captain Williams later told me that I had reported thirteen Gurkha Officers, twelve N.C.Os and a hundred and sixteen 15cwt trucks as being present on parade that morning! Although he did not believe a word of it, he realized that I was suffering from the 'morning after' and expressed the hope that I would not be led astray by the G.Os in future now that I had been given a salutary lesson in the potency of the local raksi. It was some time before I dared to touch the stuff again and when I did I made quite sure that it was well diluted with drinking water!

In the month of December 1941 I was sent off to Saugor in the Central Provinces on a Company Weapons course for three weeks and this was followed by a week's leave which I spent with my cousin, Major Hugh Travers and his wife at Ferozapore.

Hugh was Training Major of his regiment, Skinners Horse, whose depot was at Ferozapore. This was a pleasant interlude spent in the company of some typical Indian cavalry types. Amongst other activities, I was taken in hand by one of Hugh's Indian officers and given a basic lesson in the game of polo. I cannot remember much about that lesson except that we went into a deep pit. When one struck the ball towards the wall of the pit, the material with which the pit was constructed caused the ball to rebound into the middle thus enabling one to gather it up once more as if playing on a field. All very exciting but I found I had quite enough to do controlling my mount quite apart from wielding a polo stick and gathering up the ball! One 'lesson' was enough to convince both me and my instructor that I was not cut out to be a polo player! Hugh came to spend a few days with me at Bakloh and we arranged a Field Exercise based on the idea that our men would defend an area which was being attacked by Hugh's men who were at that time being trained in the use of Scout Cars. It was all very jolly and some interesting lessons were learned on both sides though I cannot remember what they were!

Whilst I was away on the course, both Robert Williams and Bill Marten were posted away to the second battalion in Egypt. I was now reasonably proficient in Urdu and had acquired a working knowledge of Gurkhali so I could now play a more active role in the Regimental Centre and was now, in my turn, an instructor for the next batch of young officers to join the regiment.

In May 1942 came a signal from GHQ calling for reinforcements. One officer was required for the first battalion in Burma and one officer was wanted for the second battalion in the Middle East. The second battalion had recently left Iraq and now formed a part of the Eighth Army in the Western Desert. Paul Messenger and I were next on the list and were summoned to the Commandant's office to be told of this latest 'offer'. As I was theoretically the senior of us by virtue of the fact that I had apparently passed out of the OTS Bangalore ahead of Paul, I was given the call of a tossed coin. I called correctly and plumped for the Middle East. It seemed to me to be the lesser of two evils. I do not like swamps, snakes or mosquitos, whereas the North African theatre of war held out the possibility of the flesh pots of Cairo and Alexandria to be sampled. Maybe in the future if one was spared, there would be the opportunity of seeing Naples and Rome and other cities to the north, assuming of course that we would eventually get there — altogether a more civilized prospect, I reasoned. I was indeed justified in my reasoning for I heard some while later that Paul was killed whilst out on patrol in Burma. There but for the Grace of God and a tossed coin would have been me.

The movement order soon arrived and I was called to the Adjutant's office to receive my orders. I was to take one NCO and forty men with me as reinforcements for the battalion which had suffered casualties in the recent advance. On further examination of the movement order a name seemed to jump out from the rest — I could hardly believe my eyes. The officer commanding the troop train was to be none other than Major T.H. Travers of Skinners Horse. The prospect of going to war with cousin Hugh could be rather fun, I thought! But little did I realize what lay ahead of me, and many a true word can be spoken (or thought of) in jest.

Preparations completed, I set off from Bakloh to Pathankot with my draft and we entrained for Amritsar where we were to transfer to the train awaiting us and bound for Bombay. I met up with Hugh at Lahore and he promptly made me his train adjutant; we thus shared a twin berth compartment. Indian trains did not have an inter-carriage corridor connection so there was a certain difficulty in maintaining contact with one's troops, I therefore put my NCO in charge of the carriage in which our forty men were travelling and hoped for the best. Hugh seemed a long time in returning. It was already six forty-five pm and the train was due to leave at six pm. Taking my duties as train adjutant very seriously I left the train to go in search of the CO and found him in the company of several of his V.C.Os (Viceroy's Commissioned Officers) having a jolly farewell party in the refreshment room. He told me not to fuss, that he had spoken to the engine driver and that he (Hugh) would be along just as soon as he could 'get away from these characters'. The party finally broke up and we were away — the time was seven twenty pm only one hour and twenty minutes late.

'Don't worry, old chap,' said Hugh, 'The war will still be on when we get there!'

The journey to Bombay lasted for two nights. During the second night some of the young Indian soldiers decided to jump train and desert as we were now passing through their own homeland where their families lived. This was duly reported to Hugh and me at the first opportunity and it was decided that, in the event of a repetition, my draft of Gurkhas should open fire through the open windows of the carriage! Just as foreseen the same thing happened. It was pitch dark outside but a further batch of soldiers had absconded. True to instructions the order was given to open fire and a fusillade of shots rang out into the blackness of the night. Whether anyone was hit I know not but it did the trick and we had no further 'escape' attempts after that!

On arrival at Bombay we reported ourselves to the RTO and told him what had happened — some thirty of our total complement were missing.

'Is that all?' he asked, seemingly amazed at the paucity of deserters. 'You've done jolly well in that case. We usually lose many more than that!'

Hugh and I shared a cabin on board the ship that was to take us to Suez. She was a pilgrim ship of a very few thousand tons, and a dry ship at that. I was despatched immediately to obtain a few bottles of whisky to keep us going — and to keep out the cold! We exercised on board as best we could and after a few days we arrived at Suez where we all went our separate ways. I and my draft were put on a train for Cairo and from there we were due to report to number eight Reinforcement Camp at Mena, quite close to the pyramids. Here we were to wait for onward despatch to our unit in the desert. Our battalion, at that time, was serving with Tenth Indian Infantry Brigade which made up a part of Tenth Indian Infantry Division.

9

Life in a reinforcement camp seemed purposeless and we did our best to keep the men happy and occupied. Route marches and lectures were interspersed with games of volley ball and soccer and we officers made occasional sorties into Cairo to relieve the monotony. Here in camp I met 'Monty' Metcalfe who had recently been commissioned from the ranks of the Devonshire Regiment. He was on what is known as the General List and was wondering what to do with himself. He had been a bandsman and was also a trained stretcher bearer so I suggested to him that he might consider applying for a posting to the Fourth Gurkhas. I reckoned he could be a useful asset. He did apply and we were to meet again later. I also met an officer from the Third Gurkhas who was awaiting posting back to his unit. I cannot recall his name but he told me a horrific story which was typical of the Gurkha's devotion to duty.

It appears that he was commanding a detachment of Gurkhas whose duty it was to guard a tent full of .303 rifles and ammunition. The tent was surrounded by a barbed wire fence and two sentries were stationed on guard — one at either side of the tent. Their brief was to patrol each side of the tent and not to permit anyone to enter and so steal the rifles and ammunition. The duty sentries were each armed with a drawn service kukri.

After supper one evening he heard a commotion and screams emanating from the direction of the arms tent. He went down to see what was happening and as he approached, the screams grew more and more faint as if receding into the distance. On his arrival at the tent, all seemed to be well. The sentry was on duty at his post at the entrance to the tent as usual. It appears that the Gurkha sentry had heard a tearing sound coming from inside the tent. He went inside to investigate and saw a hand groping through a slit in the canvas wall of the tent; the hand was obviously feeling around for rifles. Without further ado the sentry, using his drawn kukri, had severed the hand from its owner and 'the sahib could see for himself inside the tent.' Sure enough, there was the slit in the canvas wall and there on the ground was the dark-skinned right hand. The verdict was that there was an Arab at large without a right hand!

To help while away some of the spells of enforced idleness in the reinforcement camp I spent a great deal of time on the Gurkha language and I was able to enlist the help of another Gurkha officer, Robert Harris of the Seventh (I believe) Gurkha Rifles. He proved an excellent tutor and I acquired a fair degree of fluency in Gurkhali, thanks to him. As time went by there was a noticeable change in the attitude of the local Egyptian populace, taxi drivers, bus and tram conductors, waiters, shopkeepers and the like. They were becoming insolent and off-hand whereas earlier they were cheerful and obliging. Then the truth was out — Rommel's Afrika Corps was on the move towards Cairo, the British Eighth Army was in disarray and in full flight before the irresistible might of the German and Italian armies. Could this possibly be true? Surely not, yet nobody seemed to know. I and my men were ordered forward to join our unit but no sooner had we left the vicinity of Cairo and were heading northwest than we were ordered to retrace our steps and return to Mena. Enemy aircraft were everywhere, straffing roads and bombing the retreating convoys. Chaos reigned!

After a little while the full reality of what had actually happened came to be known and we learned to our dismay that our unit, the 2/4th Gurkha Rifles, together with the entire formation of which it formed a part, had been either captured or killed in action. The effect on morale was alarming — nothing is so disturbing and alarming to a young soldier than the uncertainty of where he belongs, and the news of the loss of our battalion caused a chill of bleak homelessness.

Meanwhile the base area became the scene of feverish activity. We were all organized into mobile columns and were practiced in desert marching, and were exercised over assault courses that were heartbreaking in their severity. All this time we were left wondering what would happen to us. Rumours were circulating that we would be posted to the 2/7th Gurkhas but this was no comfort. We had nothing against the Seventh but we belonged to the Fourth. Our fears proved groundless however for, a few days later, we were informed that we were to join up with the remnants of our battalion at Quasassin and that the battalion was to be re-formed. Our spirits rose immediately and in a few days we were off. The date was 2 July 1942.

Our journey to Cairo railway station was not without incident. Owing to the general situation there was no military transport available so our party was transported to the main railway station in Cairo by tram. Egyptian trams were single deckers and comprised two separate vehicles coupled together, the leading vehicle supplying the motive power. Half the party travelled in each vehicle. I had by this time acquired as my second-in-command a Gurkha Officer named Subedar Khagu Pun who was travelling in the second vehicle. All went well as far as the bridge where the main road dips under the railway line. Just as we had negotiated the dip and were climbing the other side, there was an agitated shout from the back of the leading vehicle — the coupling had parted and the rear coach was running backwards down the slope and gathering momentum at a terrific rate. Needless to say, this incident attracted the usual crowd of Egyptian spectators all of whom offered advice on the best way to re-couple the tram. After a considerable period of time during which the driver and conductor had argued with each spectator in turn, the two halves were reunited and we set off again and reached the station without further mishap. The climax of this somewhat unusual military operation occurred on arrival at the railway station when the conductor demanded that I should pay the fare! This was a poser for which I had neither budgeted nor foreseen, and no amount of argument would convince the conductor that the army would pay! I handed him over to the RTO who presumably settled the matter, and we proceeded en route to Quassassin.

10

We left Cairo, transported in open trucks, at four o'clock the next morning and joined the remnants of the battalion at about midday on 3 July where we found Major John Strickland, George Inglis and 'Dixie' Dean awaiting our arrival. My draft of some forty GORs together with Subedar Khagu Pun just about doubled the strength of the battalion and very few of us had had any battle experience whatsoever. John Strickland had been wounded in the desert and had been evacuated a few days before the disaster and Dean had managed to get out together with Jemedar Mangalsing Thapa and a few vehicles. Transport of every description had streamed to the rear in utter and complete confusion and chaos and were constantly being harried by enemy aircraft.

Needless to say the vehicles were of the utmost value and the drivers too, for they were the only specialists that we had. These latter were now suddenly become quite senior riflemen and almost all of them were soon promoted to become NCOs and were consequently lost to us as drivers. A total of four Bren Gun Carriers, fourteen three ton lorries, two fifteen hundredweight trucks, four motor cycles and two cookhouse lorries were recovered from the battle and it was on these remnants both of men and vehicles that John Strickland set about reorganizing the unit into some semblance of military unity.

Most of the remnants of the Eighth Army which had escaped from Rommel's successful advance were collected in the area and were formed into an emergency force known as 'Qatcol' and were to defend the base area in the event of enemy parachute landings. Our unit was divided into two skeleton companies. I was put in command of one of these companies with Jemedar Mangalsing Thapa as my second-in-command. Various stragglers had rejoined us by now so that the total strength of the Battalion must have been about two hundred all ranks. We were kept busy with patrols and other keep fit exercises.

On 7 July Lieutenant Colonel G.A. (Ginger) Fullerton who had previously left for India returned to take command and we soon set off for Haifa en route for Cyprus where we were to re-form and re-train.

On arrival at Famagusta in Cyprus I was detailed with several other ranks who were drivers to fetch such transport as had been allocated to us, and we rejoined the Battalion at our camp at Malounda. I was now in possession of a B.S.A motor cycle which I soon exchanged for a Matchless machine after I had had a chance to do some work on it! We eventually moved to a tented camp at Peristerona, some fifteen miles west of Nicosia, the capital of Cyprus, and on the main road to Troodos, and we were to remain there until we were moved to Italy in March 1944.

Reinforcement drafts continued to arrive from India and by the end of 1942 we were up to strength again though by no means ready for war. All our specialists had to be trained — drivers, signallers, anti-tank gunners and so forth.

Some time about the end of October 1942 I was sent off on an Intelligence Officers' Course near Cairo, to be followed by a further course in Air Photography Interpretation. These courses were good fun and I thoroughly enjoyed both of them as they appealed to the latent artistic side of my nature, and I passed both courses with flying colours. The travel arrangements both there and back were unusual and quite exciting. On the outward journey I was conveyed by air from Nicosia to Haifa in Palestine in a twin engined RAF transport plane. This was the very first time I had ever flown. On the evening of arrival at Haifa I was having a drink in the bar of the Officers' Club when I met with the pilot of the plane which had brought me over. On my thanking him for a safe flight and telling him it was the first time I had flown, he replied that I was lucky it was not the first and last time as it had been a bit 'dicey'. One engine had been inclined to cut out.

'Jolly lucky to get here actually,' he said!

Christmas 1942 was spent in Cairo where I met with another cousin, Hugh's sister Cecile, who was working with SSAFA, I believe. Then came the return journey to Cyprus. I took train for Haifa to retrace my steps but on arrival there I found there was no boat or plane bound for the island and I was directed to Beirut in Lebanon. Armed with a movement order from the RTO I took train for Beirut. The railway ran for the most part along the coast and had been built by the Canadian engineers who had had to blast their way through solid rock for many miles of the route. The RTO at Beirut was somewhat nonplussed by my request for onward passage to Cyprus but after a day or two he offered me the job of ship's adjutant on board the Royal Navy minelayer, HMS *Manxman*, which was currently engaged in transporting a battery of Gunners from Cyprus to Beirut and ferrying their relief battery from Beirut to the island. If I would do this job for him I could remain in Cyprus at the conclusion of the seventh trip. My task was to see to the orderly embarkation and disembarkation of the troops and their equipment which were housed on the decks normally used for carrying Royal Navy mines. This was a very congenial occupation. I was technically part of the ship's crew. I lived in the Ward Room where gin was four old pence per tot, I slept in a hammock slung between pipes in a corridor and enjoyed the flesh pots of Beirut every evening for a week! A Night Club called *The Dug Out* was a favourite haunt, I remember.

In January 1943 I rejoined the battalion as Intelligence Officer and held this appointment until May when I was appointed Adjutant in place of Maurice Biggs who took over a company. During my time as Intelligence Officer I set myself the task of making a complete scale plan of the battalion area which was to prove most useful. I also planned and executed a training exercise with my own section of Intelligence personnel and the Signals platoon under Oliver Nicholl. We took two fifteen hundredweight trucks and spent a weekend under canvas near Morphou practising signals procedure and Intelligence duties.

Just before taking over as adjutant I was sent to Corps HQ on a ten-day Mine Handling course and I found this course both interesting — and exciting! There were twelve regimental officers on the course which was conducted by a warrant officer from the Royal Engineers. We were taken through all aspects of both high explosives and mine handling so that by the end of our time we could distinguish the different mines and explosives, both friend and foe, and could lay a mine field and dismantle both anti-personnel and anti-tank mines. We were also taught how to inspect for and dismantle such booby traps as we were likely to come across. (It should be remembered that this was the year 1943 when explosives, detonators and such like were far less sophisticated than they are today.)

The latter part of the year 1943 was spent in advanced training and in January 1944 came the order we had all been awaiting. We were to prepare to leave the island and to proceed to Palestine where the Tenth Indian Infantry Brigade was assembling in readiness for its transportation to Italy to rejoin the war. This was a very busy time for both myself and the quartermaster. It was my responsibility to co-ordinate the transport, make out the movement orders for each company and prepare the route to the port of embarkation whilst the quartermaster had to see to the handing over of the camp to the incoming unit and also prepare indents for rations for all ranks until we were safely on board the vessel which was to take us to Haifa. The early part of the year was excessively wet and one day I had to visit Brigade HQ. All the rivers were in spate and on our return we found that the bridge over the river had been washed away by the flood water. The countryside for miles around seemed to be under water and we were forced to make a detour via Morphou. Again the surrounding country was one vast lake — somewhere through the midst of this lake ran the road marked out at intervals by metal railings which showed the line of the bridge. If one once left this line one was, quite literally, sunk!

As this was the only way home we pressed on and hoped for the best. Water was over the axles of the truck but more by good luck than good judgement we made it. I have often wondered since then what would have happened to us should we have deviated from the invisible road as there was no one in sight who could have helped us or reported our whereabouts.

Towards the end of January we proceeded in convoy to Famagusta where the Battalion embarked and sailed for Haifa and on by road to Gaza where the Division was assembling. We remained there for about two months. During this time Thirteen Corps of which our division formed a part, held a wireless and communications exercise near Cairo, so the C.O. (Ginger Fullerton), the Signals Officer (Oliver Nicholl), the Intelligence Officer (Monty Metcalfe) and myself were despatched for this caper. I can recall little about this exercise except that I had to drive the jeep all the way and it seemed a long, long way!

In March 1944 the battalion embarked on the liner *Strathnaver* and sailed for Italy, a voyage of about five days in atrocious weather, where we arrived and landed by barges at Taranto on 22 March. Taranto had had a real bashing and the harbour was littered with wrecked shipping which had been sunk by allied bombs and torpedoes as a result of a raid by Swordfish aircraft a few weeks earlier. After a week or two getting acclimatized (there had been some heavy falls of snow recently) the battalion moved up to the front line. We took over a section of the line just north of the coastal town of Ortona, where we relieved the Canadians. Battalion HQ was in a farmhouse which we shared with the farmer and his wife. The Germans used to send out fighting patrols to test our strength and on two consecutive nights we were engaged in some fierce fighting. The CO made his tactical HQ in the reserve company HQ and the enemy managed to infiltrate between our positions, and the resultant noise was deafening. We suffered our first casualties — and I was terrified!

Our Patrol platoon under Bill Tait had discovered a dry stream bed flanked by a well-worn path which he felt might have been used by the enemy during his probing patrols along our front. Our CO therefore decided that anti-personnel mines laid along this stream bed and the adjacent path would deter and quite possibly prevent the enemy from using this line of approach. He entrusted this job to me so I went out one moonlit night with a party of men from the pioneer platoon to set a minefield. During this operation we were to be covered (or protected) by Bill Tait's patrol platoon. We two British officers daubed soot on our faces and wore balaclavas against the cold and set off armed with a tommy gun each to get the job done. Where laying a minefield was concerned it was the officer's job to arm the mines when they were in position so I set my men on to digging holes and inserting the mines in the dry stream bed. This stream bed ran alongside a well worn path and was flanked by thick bushes which followed the line of the stream and the path. Whilst I was arming these mines I heard footsteps approaching from the direction of the enemy so I crept out on to the path and hid myself behind a bush. A figure appeared some six yards away. It could have been anyone. It was carrying a rifle at the ready and was wearing what looked like a German helmet. I challenged with the password. He stopped and gave the correct reply and I heard the click as he released the safety catch on his rifle. I could see by now that he was a Gurkha rifleman from the covering or patrol platoon but he could not, presumably, recognize me in the dark and with my face blackened! There we were in the middle of No Man's Land and in full moonlight, confronting each other and with our fingers on the triggers of our respective weapons! I told him I was the Adjutant Sahib. He peered at my blackened face and replied: 'No you are not the adjutant.'

I tried a conversation in Gurkhali to no avail so I started on names beginning with Captain Tait, his platoon commander, then Jemedar Motilal, his platoon second-in-command, then Havildar Tekbahadur, his platoon serjeant. I knew these names, of course, in my position as battalion adjutant and eventually I managed to persuade him of my identity so all was well and we accepted each other as friends — not foes!

Without further ado I prepared to resume my task and plunged back through the bushes into the dry stream bed. Then I froze in my tracks. How far had I got in arming those mines — and where had I scrambled out to lie in wait for those advancing footsteps? It was pitch dark amongst those bushes so, gingerly, I descended on hands and knees and felt slowly and carefully around for the tell-tale trip wires. First one — and now another — and then a third one. I was right in the middle of my own minefield! Cautiously I stepped out onto the path and tried again until I found where I had left off and so finished the job — before it finished me! I learnt afterwards that we bagged no Germans but that one of our own riflemen, out on a sniping mission, was killed on that minefield whilst he was stalking a German sniper. Such is the futility of war!

In June 1944 we left Ortona and moved across to Venafro and it was here that many of our men who had been POWs and who had managed to escape to rejoin the Battalion were hidden by the Italian peasants and helped on their way back. Many men went off to look up those families who had befriended and helped them to escape the Germans. From now on it was one hard slog northwards as the enemy withdrew from one lay-back position to another and he contested each position as we arrived so we had to fight our way forward.

Colonel Fullerton left us on 3 July as the edict had gone forth that commanding officers must be under the age of forty-two years. This was a bitter blow to the battalion as 'Ginger' Fullerton had built up the unit from scratch and had made it into a first class fighting machine. He was as fit both physically and mentally as any of his officers of half his age, and we were all very sorry to see him go. Lieutenant Colonel 'Boy' Stevenson Hamilton took over command. He seemed quite oblivious to danger of any kind. I had resumed the appointment as adjutant and it was my duty to accompany the CO on his recces. This was all very well except that he used to hare around the countryside in his jeep, leaving a cloud of dust behind him and thus providing the German gunners with an obvious target which they were not slow in engaging. Many were the 'stonks' I had to endure with the CO!

We were upset yet again when 'Boy' left us in August and Lieutenant Colonel 'Beetle' Lowis rejoined to take command. He held this appointment for the duration of the Italian campaign except when he left for home leave and Lieutenant Colonel John Stone took temporary command. A strange quirk of fate occurred in connection with John Stone's arrival to take command during 'Beetle's' absence on leave. In my capacity as adjutant I received orders from Brigade HQ to collect our new CO from the said HQ. At this time we none of us knew who the new CO would be so off I went to collect him. Imagine my surprise when I found him in the officers' mess and I can hear him now as he turned to meet me:

'Oh, good God, it's you, is it!'

11

Some time in the spring of 1945 I was posted as an instructor to the Indian Infantry Specialists School at Benevento and I was to remain there until I went on home leave in June of that year, by which time the war in Europe was over. This job as an instructor was a pleasant change from footslogging through the hills and valleys of central Italy, though I heard later that the Battalion was soon following the line of the main road north (Route 9) and was thus engaged in a series of river crossings. It was about this time that I received a letter from my mother in which she recalled the 'Winsland Blitz'. I knew nothing about this event and I give an extract from her letter as follows:

... 'Our private blitz was a year ago — it really was a hectic night. We heard the huns buzzing around and for the first time we decided to go downstairs. Daddy and I both had flu so we stayed indoors and brewed tea! Suddenly we heard a plane diving down and then there was a terrific ''bump'' as the bomb fell in the rose garden. Pa appeared from the drawing room and remarked ''all the windows have gone''. Just at that minute another Jerry had a shot at us. This happened four times and the house really rocked. Windows and frames just burst in. Soot from the drawing room fire fell like black snow over everything. When we looked out next morning there was an enormous bomb crater just by the rose garden, less than thirty yards from the house and another one in the lane just outside the front gate which completely blocked the lane. There were two more in the fields some way away. The house was bitterly cold, no windows, no frames and everyone was awfully kind offering us a home. Anyway we stayed at Winsland until the Totnes Town Council decided the best way to fill up the craters was with the Totnes refuse. Golly did it smell! We were simply driven out. What with the smell, the rats and flies! Can you imagine any town council deciding to fill craters with rotten refuse and not even put lime or earth over it — and they were still going strong after six weeks and the aroma still rose to Heaven!'

When I returned home on leave in 1945 I was able to ask my parents about that 'blitz'. It transpired that one night an enemy bomber was trying to hit a goods train that was heading for Plymouth and was, at the time, in the station at Totnes. The authorities moved the train out of the station so that it would be protected by a cutting just a few hundred yards beyond our property. The German bomber followed the train and dropped his bombs, trying to hit it. A total of five high explosive bombs, all aimed at the railway line, fell within a few hundred yards of the family home. Mother and father removed themselves to the Imperial Hotel in Exeter until such time as repairs could be effected. The local council thought the best way to fill in the crater in the lane was to use it as a rubbish tip. This was duly done and the local rat population thought that this was 'manna from heaven' and took over the whole of the district! This was when my parents decided that enough was enough and removed themselves to Exeter. Exeter, too, had had its fair share of attention from enemy bombers and fortunately there was no damage to the cathedral. A great part of the Cathedral Close and surrounding area was laid waste however. I am told that, in order to divert the German bombers away from the city, large bonfires were lit on the moorland outside in the hope that the enemy pilots would mistake these fires for the burning city centre. I believe this ruse worked for a while until the enemy got wind of what was happening.

Towards the end of June 1945 I set off for the UK and the start of sixty-one days leave. We docked at Liverpool and set foot in England for the first time in over four years. I proceeded immediately to Lime Street station for the journey to Torquay in Devonshire where my parents had taken a flat at Corbyn Head. I can recall the air of emptiness at the railway station

— there were no porters or station staff — and almost all the people around, both male and female, were in uniform: some going on leave, some just hanging about perhaps meeting girl or boy friends. The war in Europe had been over since May so there was a great deal of coming and going amongst the service personnel. The area round the railway station had not been too badly hit by enemy bombs but the dock area was devastated and presented a sorry sight to the returned 'warrior'. Soon we were on our way and I began to speculate on what I should find on arrival home, would I see a great change in my mother and father after all these years?

When I reached the flat I found a note awaiting me, for I had sent a message to tell them of my impending leave. They were on holiday at the Carbis Bay Hotel, near St Ives in Cornwall and I was to join them there. I checked with the station that there was a train to St Erth and phoned the hotel to say I was on my way. In those days one could take a train to almost anywhere in the UK so I had no difficulty in reaching my destination. There to meet me were Mum and Dad — both full of excitement at our reunion. They were just as I had left them. The intervening years had not wrought much change though Mother's hair had gone quite grey! The Carbis Bay Hotel was lovely. There was a staff to look after us, the lounge and bar were comfortable and the hotel situation was quite delightful, perched as it was right on the edge of the sea so that one could walk straight out of the hotel on to the sandy beach. There were no holiday makers such as there are today so that one had the whole stretch of beach to oneself. I remember buying a sports jacket in St Ives and the check pattern struck me as being terribly gaudy. It was, in fact, quite a normal pattern but such was the visual impact after so many years in khaki that I was quite embarrassed at the possible reaction. I also bought for my parents an original and signed water colour painting by S.J. Lamorna Birch entitled *The Looe Pool*. I have that painting in my bedroom to this day. The location of this picture has always intrigued me and about two years ago when we were on holiday in Cornwall, and staying at the Carbis Bay Hotel, Vi and I made our way down to the Looe Pool which I am glad to say is just as it is depicted in the painting, but we failed to find the spot where the artist set up his easel. I remember the price of the picture — £20! — and I presented it to Mum and Dad as a sort of coming home present.

At the conclusion of our holiday at Carbis Bay we returned to Torquay and my father invited me to drive them home. They still had dear old FWA, a black Hillman 14, registration number FWA 938, which indicated that she had first been registered in Sheffield. I believe my father bought her during our last visit to Sheffield for Christmas 1938 and the price was somewhere in the region of £180! I do know he was stopped by a complete stranger in Torquay whilst I was there on leave, and was offered £500 for the car!

To return to our journey home. All went well until we reached Plymouth where I became completely lost. I knew the town quite well from our visits there in pre-war days but now there were no familiar landmarks to be seen anywhere. Every street had been destroyed and the city centre had the appearance of utter desolation and ruin. Poor old Plymouth — the German bombers had certainly given it a pasting! Dad knew his way as he had driven through the city at least once a week in the course of his duties as Observer Group Officer with the Royal Observer Corps when he visited his posts in the southern part of Cornwall.

Incidentally, whilst we were at Carbis Bay my sister, Eve, was able to make a fleeting visit from Plymouth where she was stationed with the ATS. She was awaiting us on our return to the hotel for luncheon and I must confess I hardly recognized her in her ATS uniform. When I left home she was a sixteen year old school girl and here she was now, a plump twenty-year old young lady. The reunion was both warm and emotional for we were always close chums.

One evening I was dining at the Imperial Hotel in Torquay with the current girl friend when I was approached by an officer who asked me if I could spare a few minutes as General Slim would appreciate a word with me. I would draw the reader's attention to the wording of this request (or order) and to note the use of the words 'spare a few minutes' and 'appreciate'. These words typified the man.

General Slim, the commander of the Fourteenth (Forgotten) Army in Burma was home on leave and was staying a few days with Mrs Slim at the Imperial Hotel. He had spotted the Tenth Indian Divisional sign on my uniform and wanted to ask after some of his old comrades and friends in the Division. After introducing me to Mrs Slim I was invited to sit down with them and he proceeded to enquire after various persons whose names I have by now forgotten. General Slim had at one time been a Brigade Commander in the Tenth Indian Division. After a few minutes chat he gave me leave to withdraw, saying:

'Your party will miss you if I keep you chattering here, Good luck.'

Amongst the various 'perks' doled out to those of us on leave from the forces were petrol coupons. These came in very handy and were much appreciated by the family generally as the use of private motor cars was severely restricted by petrol rationing — in fact, I believe the public generally were forbidden to use their cars at all unless they were engaged in 'war work'.

One of our officers, Bill Tait, was killed whilst attempting to clear some enemy anti-personnel mines near Venafro. He was an enthusiastic photographer and the possessor of a very good 35 mm camera which he told me had been given to him by a friend near Brixham. I had offered to return this camera to Bill's friend as he did not live far away from Torquay. I arranged a visit one day and took the camera with me. He lent me a Triumph 250 cc motor cycle for the duration of my leave. Little did I realize that there was a price to be paid for his generosity. I was asked to a picnic party one day and discovered to my surprise that the 'party' consisted of three other men and that I was expected to strip off and be photographed in the nude in the garden! No, thank you! I withdrew hastily and returned home by bus!

Mrs Tait I found to be both welcoming and charming and I maintained contact with her for many years. I was able to tell her something of her son's career in our battalion and of our life in Bakloh, Cyprus and Italy.

My leave finished and on the appointed day I entrained once more, this time for Glasgow where I was to report to the Transit Camp for onward despatch back to Italy. After a few days hanging around we were all sent home again. There had been a mistake and we were to be moved overland to Italy now that the war in Europe was over. 'Go home and await orders.' So back to Torquay I went and eventually received a movement order to report to the Transit Camp at Newhaven. We were to be ferried across to Dieppe and thence conveyed by train to Milan in Italy. The train journey lasted about two days and I remember little of it apart from some beautiful scenery. On arrival at Milan I checked in at the Officers' Club while I endeavoured to find out where my unit was stationed as I intended to rejoin my battalion wherever it was and as soon as possible.

In order to familiarize myself with the city and its 'offerings' for those of us on leave or just passing through, I enquired of the British serjeant on duty at the Reception Desk as to what the city of Milan had to offer. I had already visited and admired the beautiful cathedral.

'Well now,' he replied, 'There's that giggley bloke singing at the hopera 'ouse.'

He was, of course, referring to that international opera star Benjamino Gigli the great Italian tenor. Alas, as luck would have it this was the last night and there were no seats to be had.

Whilst in Milan I met by chance the head clerk from Brigade Headquarters whom I knew quite well. His name was Mottram. He was on leave in Milan and he told me that my Battalion was up on the Yugoslav border keeping the peace and the whole Division was due to be shipped back to India in about six to eight weeks time. There was not much doing up there but a vacancy existed for a Staff Captain at GHQ Second Echelon which was situated near Naples. Thus I finished my tour of duty in Europe as a Staff Captain at Second Echelon, a posting which I much enjoyed as it enabled me to attend several performances of Italian opera by Italian opera singers at La Scala Opera House in Naples.

Early in October 1945 I received orders to report to my unit at Taranto prior to repatriation to India. It was here in Taranto that I received the sad news of the death of my boyhood and lifelong chum, Laugharne Richardson. He had gone right through the war as a regular officer in the Royal Marines and had died of polio in Malta where he was stationed. He was a very keen and expert dinghy sailor and was a founder member of the Maltese Yacht Club. This club instituted a trophy in his name, to be called the Richardson Trophy, to be competed for annually in his memory. It must have been devastating for his parents whom I called Uncle John and Aunt Dorothy — I had known them since childhood at Charlton Kings where our two families had first become acquainted and subsequently very close friends.

It was good to meet up with my old comrades again. We

returned to India and entrained at Bombay bound for the rail head at Pathankot. As I was not officially on strength of the battalion I was posted to the Regimental Centre at Bakloh where I was immediately promoted to Major and appointed to command the Demobilization Wing which was situated in Leslie Lines. I relieved Malcolm Gross as OC Demob Wing and was allocated number six Bungalow near to the Officers' Mess. Here was another strange coincidence — number six Bungalow was also known as 'T' bungalow after my cousin Robert Travers whose bungalow it had been after the first world war.

Hamish Mackay was commanding the Centre at this time and it was my duty to present each squad of men to Hamish before they left for home after processing through the Demob Wing. He would thank each man in turn on behalf of the 'Raj' shake their hands and wish them well for the future.

Whilst I was in the Regimental Centre I heard that my great uncle Arthur had died of typhoid fever. It was his habit to pick up a dozen oysters whenever they were available and it was assumed that it was from one of these that he had picked up the germ that killed him. This event put an entirely different complexion on my future and I wrote immediately to my grandfather who was now the sole managing director and chairman of the family business and asked him if I might join the firm on my release from the forces. He wrote back to say he would be happy for me to join the business but that I must not expect any favours either from him or from any of the senior staff. I would start at the bottom just like anyone else, (I was to wonder later on whether he did just that?). Anyway, there was a job to go to so I withdrew my application for the Colonial Service which I had submitted a few weeks earlier and had been accepted subject to interview.

It was now my turn for release (RUK32) and so, in June 1945 I left Bakloh for the last time and was driven down to the railway station at Pathankot whither I had arrived in September 1941 as a very 'green', newly commissioned second lieutenant, full of eager anticipation coupled with an overwhelming sense of awe at the prospect of joining the Fourth Prince of Wales' Own Gurkha Rifles. After all, I was but twenty-one years of age and had had no experience whatsoever of commanding men save what I had gleaned at school as a serjeant in the O.T.C. and as Head Boy of my house.

Subedar Khagu Pun who had been my subedar in the Demob Wing was there to see me off. He had suggested that he would arrange for the route out of the regimental centre to be lined by men from the Demob Wing to wave me away but I asked him not to do that. I had grown very fond indeed of the regiment and the men in it and the parting was traumatic enough without adding to the agony. I would rather slip away silently just as I had arrived all those years before — without any fuss. I made my farewells and was off, to face the future in civvy street.

12

All returned service personnel were given three months paid leave so after collecting my demobilization suit, shoes, overcoat and hat from the depot at Guildford, I headed for home in Torquay where the family was still living in their rented flat on Corbyn Head. My sister, Eve, was also demobbed about this time so the Davy family was reunited once more. My father had been elected to the Board of Directors of Arthur Davy & Sons Ltd in Sheffield now that uncle Arthur was no more, so he and I went up to Sheffield together to arrange for my joining the firm. John Willows, an ex-public schoolboy who had joined the business before the war, was asked to look out for digs for me and it was agreed that I should start my business career on the first Monday in October 1946, that I should be known as Mr Arthur and that my salary should start at £500 per annum. I was at that time drawing a salary of about £950 as a Major in the Indian Army.

I sent off my trunk in advance during the preceding week and left by train for Sheffield on Friday 28 September and was met at Sheffield Midland station by Charles Moss, the Secretary and Joint Managing Director. John Willows had found me some digs at Ranmoor Service Chambers, Nether Green which was owned and run by Mr and Mrs Gethin. Mr Gethin worked for the Sheffield Gas Company. There were about a dozen of us lodgers there on a supper, bed and breakfast basis at £2.10s.0d. per week. This may sound like peanuts today but, at £500 per annum, my monthly pay cheque was just over £41 or about £10 per week out of which was deducted Income Tax and Insurance stamp. A further drain on the exchequer was the daily tram car fare of two pence each way. I soon joined the Abbeydale Squash Club and also managed to buy and run a motor car — a 1939

Ford 10, registration number JU 9773 which I financed out of my gratuity, in the sum of £170.

John Willows who was a fairly senior executive in the firm, befriended me and introduced me to the Abbeydale Sports Club and many members of the Squash and Cricket Club sections, the two affiliated clubs in which I was especially interested and the friendships forged by Abbeydale formed the basis of my social life as an additional eligible bachelor. It is interesting to look back on the social strata that operated in Sheffield at that time. The steel fraternity and those on the periphery of that industry considered themselves a cut above the rest of us and I soon realized my position in the 'pecking' order. I had no cause to change my mind in this respect when I left the food trade for a more congenial occupation.

On presenting myself at Head Office at the appointed hour of the appointed day I was assigned to the Wages Department on the second floor under Mr Bert Thorpe. Frank Grafton was the chief wages clerk. My first jobs were to enter and total up the shops' wages for the week and to strike a balance for the retail sector. This provided a useful exercise as I soon learned the names of all the shop managers and manageresses. I also discovered that my mental arithmetic had become somewhat rusty but a few days poring over figures soon put that weakness to rights. After two weeks I was moved to the factory itself and did my time in both the meats and baking/confectionery departments. It was whilst serving my time in the factory manufacturing departments that I first had to employ subterfuge to further my 'education' in the food trade.

My grandfather who was now the Chairman, and joint Managing Director with Charles Moss who combined those duties with those of Company Secretary, summoned me to the private office-cum-Board room one day and proceeded to tell me that I was to be a spectator only and that he did not expect or desire that his grandson should engage in the practical side of factory production. How was I to know how to do things like linking sausages, decorating cakes and so forth if I had not actually done these tasks for myself? That does not matter, he told me. We employ people to do that sort of thing. Rather than argue the point I returned to the factory and posted sentries at the entrance of the appropriate departments to warn me of the approach of 'trouble'. Having thus secured my base I was able to devote my attention to learning the practical side of butchery, sausage linking and all the ramifications of the meats department as well as the mixing and moulding of dough for bread, and the various mixes for cakes and confectionery and the decoration thereof.

I must have been rather a nuisance to the Powers That Be for I was for ever asking for a move because I felt that I had mastered each particular section of the factory, for it was not long before I was given a department of my own to run. The bread despatch office was created specially for me and this consisted of a portable office complete with telephone and a salary increase of £50 per annum! It was henceforth my job to take the bread orders from the shops, pack them in hampers of three dozen per hamper and arrange for their transport to the shop concerned. I had a female clerk to assist me, Mary Bradley by name, and she would hold the fort whilst I went off to see how the warehouse functioned, how the live pigs were handled when they were delivered and so on.

At about this time, towards the end of October, my army friend, Eric Stretton, invited me to be his best man at his forthcoming marriage on Boxing Day with Sheila Anderson, in Birmingham. This invitation resulted in some cross words with my mother who pointed out to me that if I were to accept I would be away from home for yet another Christmas and that we had not had a family Christmas together since 1940 and that my sister was looking to me to be her escort over the festive season. Such was the influence that my mother had over me that I regretfully declined the invitation — and have regretted that decision ever since although I suppose it was the correct one to make. As it was I journeyed home to Torquay armed with a Davy's 2lb Pork Pie, 1lb Davy's Tomato Sausages and a Davy's decorated Christmas Cake (a D.I.Y. job, of course!).

I also received an invitation from my one-time housemaster and his wife at Malvern College, the Reverend and Mrs Cosgrove, to attend the end of term house supper. This was to be the first house supper in our old house since the college was de-requisitioned after the end of the war. During the war years the college had been evacuated, first to Blenheim Palace for about a year and then to Harrow School where the masters and boys were kindly received and where they remained until the end of hostilities. Malvern College buildings had been requisitioned by the War Office as a suitable site for the development of radar. I am told that the house dining hall housed the diesel engines which generated the electric power required for the experiments. All the dormitories' wooden partitions had been removed so that the boys now slept in communal dormitories — gone were the days (or rather nights) of privacy. I understand that this is still the case.

Whilst on this visit to Malvern I decided to motor across to Birmingham to see Eric. Alas, when about half way there, a big-end gave way in the engine of my Ford car. Luckily this occurred near a garage and I was able to leave the car there for repairs and I returned to Sheffield by train. A week later I returned to collect my car — the bill was £5!

January 1947 saw the start of one of the hardest winters that I can ever remember. I had returned from India in the previous June so I was not really acclimatized and on 21 January it started to snow. I had been through some fairly harsh weather in Italy during the war but this was something quite different. The snow was non-stop and the slush was disgusting. Snow ploughs kept the main arteries open so that those of us who had motor cars were able to remain mobile but the snag was the snow ploughs created a wall of snow in front of the entrance to one's driveway so that you had to dig your way in on return from work and dig your way out in the morning. This was the start of my personal vendetta against snow falls — I WOULD NOT be defeated!

I soon became a keen, enthusiastic but somewhat indifferent performer on the squash court and I had a regular date with a stockbroking friend, Jim Booker. We played squash every Thursday evening after which we went to his home where his wife, Pam, had a meal ready for us, after which we would listen in on the radio to that truly British institution ITMA featuring Tommy Handley. My other regular squash 'opponents' were Robert Gray and Peter Wild.

My parents had, by this time, moved north from Torquay and rented the Home Farm, Firbeck near Worksop and I had changed my 'digs' from Ranmoor to Millhouses. This latter move came about through Peter Stone whom I had got to know in the Territorials. The local territorial battalion (The Hallamshires) were re-formed under Lieutenant Colonel J.P. Hunt. I felt at the time that it might be good policy to join them as I missed the camaraderie of Mess life. I offered myself and was accepted as a Captain (my substantive rank) and appointed as second-in-command B Company under Major Mike Lonsdale Cooper. I was also appointed Messing Officer presumably because of my connection with the food trade. One of my duties in this capacity was to compile and submit to the local food office the number of main meals, beverages etc served and consumed in the Officers' Mess. Serjeant Frost and his wife ran the Mess and were responsible for the catering and general upkeep of the building and very efficient they were too. Conscription was in operation and after their spell with the colours all conscripts were expected to do a tour of duty with their local territorial unit. It fell to my lot to give a lecture and then to interview each man afterwards. This event was duly reported in the local evening paper, complete with photograph.

Whilst on demob leave in Torquay I became acquainted with Margaret Anderson whose sister ran a private car hire business in London, from her flat just off Ebury Street. Margaret was a State Registered Nurse and I spent many weekends in London, staying at the Goring Hotel which was almost opposite the Anderson flat. Looking back over these past years I realize now that I was in love with Margaret but such was my naivety and inexperience with the opposite sex that my courtship led to nothing. She got a nursing job in Bournemouth looking after an elderly widower and many were the telephone calls I put through from Sheffield just to talk to her but eventually we lost contact. After a long pause she did write to me suggesting we resume our relationship but the passage of time had killed my feelings for her and so I replied declining the suggestion. I had by now met Gilly Chesterman at a tennis party given by Lord and Lady Manvers at Thoresby Hall, near Worksop. Gilly was great fun and we had many interests in common. She and her sister were orphans and lived with their guardians, Mr and Mrs Anthill at Worksop. Mr Anthill was Secretary of James Chesterman & Sons, small tool manufacturers in Sheffield.

Whitsun 1947 saw my first cricket tour with the Sheffield Collegiate Cricket Club to Devonshire. The Devon Tour was an annual event. The team stayed at the Grand Hotel in Plymouth from whence matches were played against the RNE College, the United Services (a two-day match) and the RN College, Dartmouth. We then moved to Sidmouth and stayed at the Belmont Hotel for matches against the Devon Dumplings (my old club) at Exeter, Exmouth and Sidmouth. It was whilst playing against the Dumplings that I found the record of the last match I had played with them in their score book. It was the match against Chiswick Park in 1940 when I took seven wickets for twenty-two runs — and Dennis Browne was in the opposing team. I was very much the new boy and kept myself to myself and enjoyed the cricket! Sport figured prominently in my social life during those days of 1947, whilst at work I did a spell at our Fargate premises where I was attached to the Cafe/Restaurant together with the making of chocolates, tasting, blending and buying of tea and coffee and the day-to-day running of the retail provision store.

About a week before Christmas 1947 I was stricken with pneumonia. One evening I had been asked out to dine at the Prisoner of War Camp at Lodge Moor, near Sheffield. I felt fine during dinner and it was not until I was making my way home later that evening that I suddenly developed a high fever and a splitting headache. The world swam before my eyes and I can remember little of the car drive home. That night I was in torment with an acute pain in my chest and a raging temperature.

Come the morning I was quite unable to stir so I sent a message to the office and summoned the doctor. My own doctor, John Connell, was unavailable so I was visited by his deputy who pronounced an attack of pleurisy and instructed me to stay in bed for a few days. My parents came to see me and a second opinion was called for. Pneumonia was diagnosed and I was rushed off to a Nursing Home at Nether Edge where I remained for about ten days. By this time Gilly Chesterman had departed to London and I was dating Mary Tonbridge from Hathersage. Mary used to come in by bus to see me nearly every day and when I was discharged I was invited over to stay with the Tonbridges to convalesce in the country. The fresh country air did me a power of good and I was soon restored to full health again — and got myself engaged to Mary into the bargain! When I returned home my mother said she hoped I might be engaged so I told her that I was. She seemed to be very pleased and when I told her that I had not yet got around to getting an engagement ring for Mary she promptly dived into her jewel box and got out a beautiful sapphire and diamond ring which she gave to me and told me that it had been her grandmother's engagement ring. As time went on I began to realise that I had made a mistake over my engagement. Mary was a very sweet and pleasant companion but gradually it dawned on me that we were not really suited to one another and that our life together would be a disaster. Our two family's lifestyles were very different and therefore our backgrounds would be similarly diverse. The engagement was subsequently broken off and she generously returned the ring. I can remember the occasion so very vividly because there was a Test Match on at Leeds and I went over there to try and forget the whole affair. Easier said than done! I was beginning to feel I must be somehow different from other young men and that maybe I was not cut out for marriage. I therefore tried to forget all about the opposite sex and flung myself wholeheartedly into cricket.

Mother had arranged for us all to go over to stay with cousins in County Cork in the Irish Republic in August so off we went there. The cousins were the Travers of Timoleague House and we travelled to Cork by the SS *Kenmare* from Liverpool. The good ship *Kenmare* was a cattle boat that plied between Cork and Birkenhead on a weekly run. She sailed outward with a miscellaneous cargo of freight and passengers and returned with a load of cattle on the hoof which she off-loaded at Birkenhead after discharging her passengers at Liverpool. Eaton Travers was at the dockside to meet us and drive us out to Timoleague, some sixty miles away. On our way out of Cork city we had to make a right hand turn off the main street on to the main road out of the city towards the towns of Bandon and Timoleague. As we turned I noticed a policeman (or Garda as they are called in Ireland) talking to someone on the pavement. As we rounded the bend the Garda blew his whistle and gesticulated to us to pull into the side of the street. He came up to my cousin's side window and exclaimed:

'Oh, 'tis you, Colonel. Do you know you came round the corner on the wrong side of the road?'

'No, I didn't know that,' replied Eaton.

'Well you did, so you did. You should go round me,' said the Garda.

'But you weren't there,' said my cousin.

'That makes no difference. You should go round me whether I'm there or whether I'm not!' replied the Garda.

That was my first introduction to Irish logic and many more cases manifested themselves as time went on.

On arrival at Timoleague House I found that I had been allocated a 180 lb tent in the garden as my sleeping quarters. This tent was loaned to them by another Travers relation, Lloyd Travers by name, and was erected in the 'Ballygarden' — the word 'Bally' is a common place in Ireland and means 'Townland'. Timoleague House was a fairly new house, built on a site adjacent to the old Timoleague Castle. The original house had been burned down by the IRA during the 1920 'Troubles' and had been situated in the area now occupied by the stables. There was a large lawn in front of the house and the avenue or driveway ran round the side of this lawn so that any vehicle approaching the house was visible to the occupants. Just outside the main gate was the Protestant Church, built on Travers land, and the village of Timoleague lay just beyond the front gates. The Travers family considered themselves the squires of the neighbourhood and seemed to us to be in constant conflict with the Bishop of Cork in whose diocese the church was situated. The Travers family seemed to be able to pick a quarrel with the Bishop over almost anything and I began to wonder whether this was a normal way of life in Ireland, for it was a well-known fact that religion played a strong part in the day-to-day conduct of affairs. Mrs Travers, my cousin Doris, was treated with the utmost respect in the village and whenever we had cause to enter the village for shopping or any other reason it was rather like a royal procession with Doris Travers raising her hand in gracious acknowledgement of the greetings of the villagers! In fact I had never come across anything quite like this before and likened it to the feudal system that I had read about in history books at school!

My cousin Eaton who was retired from the Royal Artillery, was a hard-working landowner and was busily engaged in trying to restore the family estates to what they had been in days gone by. On his retirement he had taken a correspondence course in Agriculture and now ran a large milking herd of Red Poll cattle as well as many acres of corn which he managed himself with the aid of four men on the farm. There were two men by the name of 'Johnny' — one worked in the garden and was known as The Mistress's Johnny. Garden produce consisting of tomatoes, lettuce, beans, and peas etc were sold direct from the garden to persons who called for their local produce. Doris was also a keen and accomplished amateur watercolour artist and she and I would occasionally disappear together to indulge our mutual interest.

One day whilst in the village I was seen with my sister by a neighbour and his sister who were driving past us in their car, and it was the neighbour's sister who was to be my future wife! One afternoon we were all asked down to Lisheen by Janie de Courcy Meade to play tennis. Janie was an aunt of the Scott children who lived at The Glen, near to Harbour View. Whilst watching the tennis and indulging in polite small talk with our fellow guests, I observed a golden-haired, sun-tanned girl playing in a ladies' four. I had not been introduced to her and resolved to make her acquaintance during the tea interval which was due shortly. Alas for the best laid plans! Tea was duly announced and I together with three other males were organized into a men's four to play tennis, after which we could adjourn for tea ourselves. I do not believe my mind was on my game for, immediately our game was finished, I was off in search of the young lady! Try as I may I was unable to establish contact with my quarry until the time came for our departure when I was able to get an introduction. I had in the meantime been able to discover that she was Mary Scott, a niece of our hostess, that she was unmarried and unattached, and that she was the younger daughter of a well respected but impecunious protestant farmer who lived and farmed at The Glen. The source of all this useful information? None other than Mary's brother, Ted! Was my face red! Anyway I had my information so it was now up to me and we saw quite a lot of each other before I had to leave for home at the end of my fortnight. This all happened in July. In the following September I was due to leave for Denmark where I was to be attached to P & S Plum (Plumrose), the Danish manufacturers of table delicacies and with whom our firm did a lot of business. The arrangement was that one of their employees did a spell with our firm on an exchange basis. Whilst in Denmark I took the opportunity of writing to Mary ostensibly to tell her and her family all about life in Scandinavia but there was, of course, an ulterior motive which was to keep in touch and develop our acquaintanceship. I had begun to realize that Mary was the girl for me — she was a country girl for a start with no high and mighty ideas, she enjoyed swimming and tennis and was tolerant of my cricket interests, she had done a spell in HM Forces as a WRN and was (so I was told) a good cook! In addition to all these virtues she was not used to the high life nor was she blessed with wealth. All these factors were in her favour so far as I was concerned because I was far from wealthy myself although I did consider my prospects were reasonably good and I would be able to give her a fair standard of living — but all in good time. Thus we maintained contact throughout the following year and then the question of our summer holiday for 1949 came up for consideration.

Meanwhile, back at work, I was still a dogs body and was now holding down the exalted title of 'Personal Assistant to the Managing Director'. I shared an office with John Smith, the manager of the Meats Department and this was next door to the Managing Director. My duties consisted of answering letters of a mundane nature, ready for Charles Moss to vet for typing and signature, writing reports for the Board of Directors on subjects to be discussed at the next Board Meeting — these reports were chiefly concerned with purchases of a capital nature such as new vans, alterations to certain shops etc and I was also in charge of the firm's advertising in the local press (*The Sheffield Telegraph*) once a month. I had twelve printing blocks made by a local firm of engravers, Eadon Engraving Ltd, depicting various aspects of the firm's business such as Bread, Cafe/Restaurants, Tea & Coffee, Cooked Meats and so on. These duties left me with a considerable amount of time on my hands so I suggested that an 'In House' Magazine would be a good thing to have published. I had seen such a magazine in other firms — Carrs of Carlisle for instance, used to send us their magazine every three months and I was given the go ahead on the same basis with a ceiling of £100 per quarter. This kept me busy and I was also able to make a closer acquaintance with all the shops and factory departments. Loxleys the Printers were responsible for printing the magazine and a competition was held throughout the firm to choose a title. A prize of £5 was offered, with £2 for the runner-up. Out of a great number of entries, the name finally chosen was *Table Topics*. This magazine ran for five to six issues until finally the Powers That Be decided that it was becoming too expensive and was not justified. I did not agree with this viewpoint but I did learn a lot about the out-of-town side of the business. The then

Managing Director never went out to visit the shops apart from his daily visit to the Fargate restaurant for his luncheon! I always felt there was a useful gap here which should be filled but although I did try to broach the subject I was always shot down and, to this day, I am inclined to blame great-aunt Alice, my great-uncle's widow, who was on the Board and was obviously jealous of my grandfather and the fact that the only male line of 'inheritance' went through him. She was, I believe, aided and abetted in this attitude by both Victor Bibby and Brian Pye-Smith. The former was the father of Colin who married Muriel, my grandfather's daughter by his second marriage and it seemed strange that such a man could father such a nice son! Brian Pye-Smith on the other hand was my great uncle's solicitor and both these gentlemen together with Charles Moss had perfected the art of 'running with the hare and hunting with the hounds'. This was the feeling I had when trying to make my way in the firm and, of course, my father was handicapped by the fact that he had been kept out of the business by Uncle Arthur so his widow was able to continue that same policy. Aunt Alice was a strong personality and was one of those persons who was able to create a situation by word of mouth and then sit back and await developments. My father was further handicapped by the fact that he had had no experience whatsoever with the business until after the war when Arthur Davy had died, when he was immediately offered a seat on the Board by my grandfather. He accepted this post and, on more than one occasion, he told me:

'I am keeping a seat warm for you, my boy.'

During the previous year I had purchased a Hillman Minx car with a sunshine roof. The roof leaked so I decided to sell the car and my father made me an offer of some ordinary shares in the firm in exchange for the money I got for the car! He said he could do with the money to clear his overdraft at the bank! I thus became a CAPITALIST with 800 x £1 , shares in the family firm! I bought a new Royal Enfield motor cycle with the balance of cash and this machine kept me mobile for getting out to the Squash Club that winter.

Some time around this time my sister who was working in London for the Official Car Services and who shared a flat with another girl, came home for the weekend feeling very unwell. Her malaise was diagnosed as appendicitis so she was hurried into hospital to be operated upon. I was deputed to go up to London and collect her car and to bring back all her belongings as she would not be returning to her job there. She was due to take over as 'Queen Bee' of the OCS in Sheffield. There was no way of contacting her flat mate. There was a telephone for the use of the tenants but no one answered my calls so up to Town I went armed with a key to the flat, a key to her car which was a sporty MG and a letter from Eve to her flat mate. I found the flat and as there was no one at home I let myself in, wondering what Eve's flat mate would say or do when she discovered a strange man ransacking the place! I had taken the precaution of getting Eve to write a note to her flat mate explaining the circumstances and introducing me as her brother who had her permission to collect her belongings and very glad I was to have this letter of introduction as the lady in question was very suspicious of me and would, I am sure, have summoned help to have me forcibly ejected! Anyway, all was well and I was able to accomplish my mission without mishap.

During the winter months I had struck up an acquaintanceship in the office with another employee named Mr Beaumont who was a walking enthusiast and who went every year for his holidays to the Lake District, staying at Grasmere. Such was the power of his description of The Lakes and their surroundings that I who had never been there was completely sold on the idea of a holiday there myself. I would go there this summer on my motor cycle — all on my own. I would do what I liked, go where I liked, see what I liked. Therefore when the subject of the family holiday came up at home I announced that I had made other arrangements and would not be going to Ireland with them. At the same time I wrote to Mary and told her of my plans. There was a long delay before her reply came. In it she expressed her disappointment at my decision, hoped I would have a nice time, looked forward to seeing my parents and sister again and that was all! I promptly changed my mind and decided to accompany the family to Ireland. Looking back after all these years I now know that I was scared stiff of meeting with Mary again, that I was in love with her and frightened of facing up to the inevitable, having made at least two abortive relationships with girls. I need not have worried. We slipped into an easy relationship and I knew that I was 'hooked!' This was July 1949 — a time of filial relationships between parents and sons; when affairs of the heart were conducted according to a strict set of rules, when children considered their parents' feelings and attitudes and when it was customary, unlike the present day, to obtain the consent of the girl's father and also, for that matter, discuss with one's own parents the wisdom or otherwise of asking one's beloved to marry one. This convention was soon to be superseded by a different set of rules whereby parental control became 'de riguer' and one's young people set no store by or for the feelings or 'wisdom' of their parents. For my own part and as I have indicated before, I held my parents in great respect and would not knowingly do anything to hurt them. I feel this may have had a restrictive bearing on my own attitudes to life and living, for I know I was reluctant to pursue my own instincts as regards personal ambitions. If I had continued my career abroad things might have been different but as soon as the war was over and I came once more under mother's influence, I became as putty in her hands except for certain occasions — but more of that anon.

One sunny afternoon the ladies went off to the tennis club, leaving my father and me at home, to laze in deck chairs in the sunshine. I had been asked to The Glen for tea and I remember asking my father what he thought of Mary and would he and mother have any objections to my asking Mary to marry me. I had had twelve months to think it over and now that I had met her again I had become convinced that she was the right girl for me. After asking a few pertinent questions as to what interests we had in common and so forth, he gave me his blessing, assured me that mother would have no objection and wished me luck when I told him I intended to ask Mary for her hand in marriage if the opportunity presented itself that afternoon. Armed with parental consent I went to The Glen for tea. Tea was served in the dining room with their maid, Mary Holland, or Hollie as she was called by the family, resplendent in cap and apron doing the honours and taking round the tea cups as they were poured by Mrs Scott. Mary's brother, Ted, and her sister, Betty, were also present and a very relaxed gathering it was. I had cause which was completely out of character, to comment on the delicious coffee cake and was told that Mary had made it — another plus mark in her favour!

It was a beautiful summer's day and as soon as we reasonably could, Mary and I suggested we might go for a walk. Ted and

Betty said they would come too, so off we all went, down to the cross roads and out along the coastal fields past the slipway. As we walked I noticed that the other two lagged behind and soon Mary and I were alone. We struck left across the road and Mary said we could make our way back across the fields. This we proceeded to do until we came to a hay field full of cocks of hay. This seemed as good a spot as any so we sat down under a hay cock and it was there that I summoned the courage to ask her to marry me. To my intense delight — and relief — she said she would and I remember little else of that evening except that there was a cow calving in the next field! We returned to The Glen much later on and the house was in darkness. I told Mary I would be back the next morning to ask for her parents' consent and set off for Timoleague. All was in darkness at the house apart from a light burning in my parents' room. Thither I went and told them my news. They seemed pleased and at breakfast next morning I was greeted with great back slappings and general good wishes. The household staff knew all about it for, unknown to us, in the field next to 'our' hay field was a cow calving and one of Mr Scott's men was in attendance. He had observed us, put two and two together and spread the information amongst his cronies in the village. Our secret was no secret at all!

The next day I presented myself at The Glen for an interview and was kindly received by Mr and Mrs Scott. I was closeted with Mr Scott in the drawing room and all I can remember of the 'interview' was a rather halting address by me in which I tried to give as good account of myself as possible, and an equally halting expression of permission from her Dad. Anyway, all was well and I was accepted as a suitable consort for their daughter. After that, Mary and I arranged a visit to Cork the following day to buy an engagement ring — my bank balance at that time stood at roughly one hundred pounds!

My cousin Doris immediately put in hand arrangements for an engagement party. Wine was procured and put to keep cool in the Well in the stable yard for there was no refrigerator in the house. Such essentials were not commonplace in Irish houses in those days. Various friends were summoned to the party fixed for that evening. Mary and I went off to Cork the next day to buy the ring and Doris gave me the names of two firms where she was well known and who would allow us to take a ring on approval. This we did. We went first to Mangans where we selected a three-stone diamond ring and then to Brennans where we were offered a diamond and zircon ring. We brought both rings home with us though I think we both knew which one we would rather have. The family agreed and we settled for the diamond and zircon ring. The other ring we returned the following day. The cost of that engagement ring was £60! There were several friends and relations round and about who all seemed delighted at our news and we were entertained royally by all and sundry. Then came the question of the Wedding Day. Doris announced firmly that it could not possibly be in Lent and that her son, Neil, must be home from school to act as an usher. I had to return to duty the next day as my two weeks holiday was up so I left the three families to sort it all out. It struck me at the time that the two persons most concerned seemed to have no say in the matter at all!

In 1950 I was told by friends that a good, solid house was soon to come on the market in Stumperlowe Crescent, Fulwood. It was a semi-detached house and the other half was owned and occupied by Tennant· and Peg Rankin. Tennant was a stockbroker with Nicholsons, stockbrokers of Sheffield. I decided to buy the house for £3,750 and the next problem was how to finance the purchase! The house had been owned and occupied by an elderly lady and her companion/housekeeper so the decor was far from serviceable. The kitchen walls for instance were thick with grease and all the woodwork was of a dark chocolate brown colour. There were two shallow earthenware sinks, one in the kitchen and the other in the scullery which led off the kitchen. There was also an old cast-iron range in an alcove in the kitchen. The walls of the staircase were papered in a heavily embossed and pinkish coloured paper and in the drawing room was a Victorian fire surround, heavily carved and with a large and protruding overmantle-cum-mirror. The entire house was uncarpeted and uncurtained and all that was left was the linoleum in one of the bedrooms and on the hallway and kitchen floors. There was a cellar, a central hallway off which led the drawing room, a dining room and the kitchen. There was also a very small cloak room, just wide enough to slide in and hang one's hat and coat! On the other side of the wall of this cloak room was an outside lavatory with a doorway leading into it from the garden. On the first floor were two double bedrooms and one single bedroom, a bathroom and a separate lavatory. Upstairs again to the attic were two further bedrooms and a box room. As my mother remarked when I showed her the house:

'Well, you will have plenty of room to expand!'

Outside was a small front garden at the side of which ran the approach path from the front gate to Stumperlowe Crescent. A gate at the side of the house led through to the rear garden which was completely neglected and gave the appearance of a jungle. At the far end of the rear garden was a metal garage, slowly disintegrating with rust and this garage was approached by a private lane down which were the garages and back entrances to four other houses. Mary was unable to come over to inspect the house but she was well aware of the areas around the West End of Sheffield and I gave her a description of the house before committing us to the purchase. The problem of finance was eased by my parents who agreed to provide us with a mortgage, out of their Marriage Settlement, of £2,000! I got a bank loan of £1,000 and managed to raise the balance myself. On the strength of my forthcoming marriage my salary was raised to £650 per annum, almost £55 per month — riches indeed! I now set to work to make pelmets for all the windows, these I made from timber at the tops and sides and hardboard fronts suitably embossed with decorative fascias. Meantime I gave Mary the measurements of the windows and after we had decided on the colour schemes for the rooms, she made up the curtains at home — and they fitted after slight adjustments to length for which she had made allowances.

Our Wedding Day was fixed for us for 14 April 1950 — the Friday after Easter — and we were to travel over to Ireland via Liverpool and Dun Laoghaire on Tuesday, 11 April. Mother and father both went down with influenza the previous week and retired to a Nursing Home to recover, having been prescribed champagne by the family doctor! Fortunately they were up and about, if somewhat limp, by the day of departure. So off we went, mother and father, and my sister Eve who was to be the principle bridesmaid, and Arthur Colver, my best man. We were met at Cork station by Mary and Ted and arrived in good order at Timoleague House where Arthur immediately went off to view the railway line which at that time was still intact and which ran past and very close to the house. Others

from England who had accepted invitations to our wedding were
Robert and Liz Gray who were our neighbours in Whiteley
Wood Road in Sheffield and Jock and Mary Anderson. Jock
Anderson was the Medical Officer from the Hallamshires and
was also a much respected and leading surgeon at the Royal
Hospital in Sheffield. The Andersons had a farm in Lincolnshire
whither they went every weekend. These two families were to
stay at the Courtmacsherry Hotel, across the estuary from
Harbour View.

Final arrangements for our wedding were made on the
Wednesday and Mary and I visited the rectory for a pre-marital
talk from the rector, Jimmy Fleming, who was to marry us.
In accordance with convention, I did not see Mary on the
Thursday and on Friday I was driven to Rathclaren Church
by Eaton Travers in time for the wedding service at one pm.
I should add here that we were due to catch the overnight ship
from Cork to Fishguard to spend the first week of our
honeymoon at the Charing Cross Hotel in London and the ship
sailed at six pm sharp. Transport had been arranged for us to
leave The Glen at four pm after the reception. The little church
of Rathclaren had been beautifully decorated for the occasion
by Mary's younger brother, Pat, who was at that time a partner
in a firm of architects in Dublin. He was also a gifted artist and
was making a name for himself in this field. He was shortly to
give up his architectural career in favour of art, though he was
still to remain on the firm's books as a consultant. I remember
the church was a mass of flowers and fern and there was a breathtaking arch half way down the centre aisle made up of apple
blossom. The toast to the Bride and Groom was given by Dr
Ormie Welpley who was not only the family's doctor but also
an old family friend. I found out later that it was almost entirely
due to Dr Welpley's attention that my future mother-in-law
made it to the wedding, as she suffered severely from heart
trouble and it was touch-and-go whether she would stand up
to all the excitement. As it was, Mrs Scott was in tremendous
form and came through the ordeal with flying colours. I recall
Dr Welpley referring to me as a 'cricket man' and as one who
had descended on their tranquil neighbourhood and made off
with one of their eligible maidens. In my reply I put him right
on the cricket man and substituted cricketer, and apologized
for my temerity in stealing one of their young ladies, and advised

them to take more care in future!

We left the reception at four pm and were driven to Cork by Philly Holland of Timoleague. The usual pranks were played on us and a tin bath was fixed by a long rope to the back of the car and the bath hidden in the bushes. We were told afterwards that we nearly had Aunt Linda for company on our honeymoon as she was standing in direct line with the bath as we were driven off! The car itself was daubed with slogans such as 'Just Married'. When we arrived at the Innisfallen we were shown to the special cabin that had been reserved for us and then we discovered to our dismay that one of Mary's hand cases was missing and had been left behind at The Glen. Just as we were congratulating ourselves on having got aboard without giving away the fact that we were just married, there was a knock at the door and in came the stewardess bearing the missing case to which was tied an old shoe! Our secret was out! The case was discovered just after we had left and Pat Vernon, a friend of the Scott family, had volunteered to rush it to us in his sporty Riley motor car. He arrived with just five minutes to spare! The journey to London passed without further mishap and two weary travellers arrived at Paddington Station at about eleven am the following morning.

Before we left The Glen we had arranged for a firm of Removers in Cork, named Nat Ross, to come in and pack up those of our wedding presents which were at The Glen and have them conveyed to Sheffield. Meantime Aunt Linda had given to Mary a Georgian Mahogany breakfast table and five Cherry Wood chairs from her furniture store in London. Also she had given us the pick of her other furniture which was also in store which we could have at pre-war valuation. We were to contact her old house keeper, Murie, and arrange a visit to the repository where the furniture was kept. This we did and chose several articles of use and value amongst which were two lovely antique Plate Buckets as well as a fine mahogany Tallboy, two mahogany chests of drawers and various other more mundane items. I sent Aunt Linda the list of the items we had selected and she generously arranged for them to be valued as at pre-war valuation and then gave me six months to pay for them. The total cost was seventy pounds! I duly sent her a cheque each month for twelve pounds and she let me off the final two pounds! Even the twelve pounds each month was quite a hardship out of my monthly salary as we were trying to set up house 'on a shoe string' and we had the entire house to decorate! Carpets were non-existent so we clattered about on bare floorboards — but it did not matter. We were in love and setting up our first home together — and what fun it all was! Then came the first blow: a telegram from her brother told Mary that her mother had passed away. This was a sad blow to me too as I hardly knew my mother-in-law. I do believe however she died a happy woman, knowing that her daughter was safely married and provided for. I hastened home from the office and arranged for us to travel over to The Glen for the funeral. Afterwards I returned home, leaving Mary to see that her elderly father was all right. After about a week she returned home herself, not without some prompting from me who had to remind her where her home was. I was lonely, too!

Soon after her return home and after a visit to the doctor of which I was unaware, she announced that she was expecting our first child. This was exciting news indeed!

One evening on my return home I found a new Indian carpet spread on the drawing room floor. Mary told me that there was nothing to worry about and that we had it on approval for a week! That was all very well but how was I expected to pay for it? Not to worry, I was told, if we cannot afford it, or if we do not like it, we can return it. And anyway, it was only thirty-two pounds — Thirty-two pounds?!! Of course, even after one evening it proved a delight to have a carpet on the floor so off I went to Walsh's to ask if I might have credit for six months to pay for it! Mr Arthur Davy of Arthur Davy & Sons asking for time to pay out thirty-two pounds for a carpet! I did not care, we wanted that carpet! The credit was sanctioned so down I went every month with my cheque for six pounds. Thus at the end of six months that carpet had cost me an extra four pounds — a total of thirty-six pounds. My father got wind of that transaction and gave me a parental telling off.

'My boy,' he said, 'if you cannot pay for something, you cannot afford it. Whatever you do, do NOT get into debt. Save up for whatever you need.'

Such was the gist of parental advice in the year 1950. How different from today when homes are fully furnished before you move in and if you need (or want) something you borrow without any thought of the morrow! Anyway, all went well and I paid off the debt.

We used to get our new-laid eggs from the Andersons every Monday when they came back from their Lincolnshire farm so we got to know them very well. In 1951, Jock was elected President of the Caledonian Society and they invited Mary and me to join their presidential party on Burns' Night at the Cutlers Hall in Sheffield. This was a great 'do' and we all enjoyed ourselves, wining and dining with the best of 'em. Sometime about midnight I missed Mary who was beginning to show signs of her pregnancy. Mary Anderson eventually found her in the ladies loo whither she had retired feeling woozy and faint from the heat.

All went well thereafter and our first born son was safely delivered at Sherwood Nursing Home in Sheffield at five twenty pm on 13 March 1951. My sister had been called to take Mary to the nursing home during the course of the afternoon and I know the time to be five twenty pm because I had just looked at my watch and felt something had happened. This occurred as I was returning home on the bus and shortly after my arrival home the telephone call confirmed my suspicions. We had arranged for the midwife, Nurse MacDonald, to attend Mary and she was to accompany her and her baby home after two weeks and to stay with us for a further two weeks to 'get us going' with our new arrival. I must say this was an excellent arrangement. We could sleep through the nights and Nurse Mac would school the new mother in the mysteries of baby care. I, as the new father, was not privy to these matters and I left each morning to continue earning our living.

One great regret I have over this event is that my grandfather, or Funny Grandad, died in February aged eighty years, about a month before our first born arrive. I had been looking forward to his becoming a great grandfather — and felt cheated by his opting out before the event.

Arthur Eaton Davy, 1945

"We Three"

E.R. Davy	A.E. Davy	E.P. Davy
Grandfather	Self	Father
	Parent's Match 1934	

My Maternal Grandfather
Brigadier General J.O. Travers CMG, DSO

Me and my sister Eve — 1925

My Paternal grandparents' Wedding Group — 1896

My wedding with Mary Scott — 1950

E.P. Davy Mrs. G. Scott   P.S. Scott Mrs. J. Davy

Aviation Française.

ANDRINOPLE

Je Soussigné Olivier certifie que le 25 8bre 1913
à Héliopolis Mlle Travers a reçu à
bord du ·Balkanic· le Baptême de l'Air en
effectuant à la hauteur de 100 mètres un
Voyage de Quinze kilomètres.

Le Pilote.   Les Témoins.

I believe that Mother was the first woman to have flown in
an aeroplane in Egypt — this was her certificate.

The Invitation to the "DINING IN" Ceremony.
This invitation posed a problem — etiquette demanded that
it should be accepted 'Officially' but for what meal was the
invitation issued.

The Officers 4th P.W.O. Gurkha Rifles

request the pleasure of the company of

Mr. A.E. Travers Davy

at Wednesday — at 8.30 o'clock

on Wednesday the 24th September 1941

R.S.V.P. to the Mess President.

My Parents — 1958

Joan Davy
and Willie

Ernest (Jack) Davy

My Mother — Joan Olive Brandreth Davy — 1938

Relaxing somewhere in Italy — 1944

Arthur Cederic Davy, my great-uncle

One of the earlier Sheffield Tramcars

The invitation to the 313th Cutler's Feast, Sheffield — 1949

Greeting the Captain and Officers on board the M.V. Oceanos — 1979

Fancy Dress Night — An 'Irish' Wedding. We won 2nd Prize!

My Grand Children 1990.
Left to right: Top
Maria (8) Craig (8)
Laura (4) Barbara (6)

13

During this period I was still employed at Head Office as a general dogsbody but soon after grandfather's death it was suggested that I might like to enter the retail side of the business. I jumped at this suggestion so, after some deliberation, I was sent down to our Castle Street branch to study the retail side of the business under Mr James Barker, one of our oldest and more experienced managers. Jimmy Barker had been with the firm ever since he was a lad and was now in his sixties. I suppose he must have been due for retirement in a few years. He had a great regard for the Davy family and seemed very pleased, and honoured, to have been selected to school the youngest Davy in the art of salesmanship. I well remember his words of advice on my reporting for duty on my first day at Castle Street branch.

'Now, Mr Arthur,' he said, 'I'll tell thee one thing, and one thing only. It's customers that pays thy wages.'

I was then handed over to the shop foreman, Bill Faulding, and put down in the cellar where I had to bone out sides of bacon, cut off and bone out hams and collars, and when I had finished that, there were more sides of bacon and also cheeses, though rationing was still in force and cheeses were limited.

After a month I was allowed upstairs and was put on the rations counter under Miss Bateman where I was initiated in the mysteries of ration books, and how to deal with awkward customers who wanted more than their entitlement. I was full of enthusiasm and was determined to show these people how to sell. One day a certain Mrs Robinson came into the shop and presented herself at the ration counter with her five ration books. The rations per person at that time consisted of two ounces of butter, four ounces of margarine, two ounces of cooking fat, one egg, and four ounces of bacon as well as a ration of sugar, sweets, etc. As each customer purchased their entitlement of foodstuffs, the retailer was responsible for removing the appropriate coupons from the ration book and, at the end of the month, sending these coupons in to the Food Office. The amount of rationed articles that each firm received for resale depended on the quantity of coupons returned to the Food Office.

After concluding the purchase of the rationed goods, Mrs Robinson then proceeded to expand upon her order and, amongst the other things she asked for was a packet of Green's Sponge Mix. As nothing else seemed to be in her mind I started my sales patter:

'Are you going to make a sponge cake, madam?' I asked.

'Aye, I am an' all. And tha' can cut out tha' bloody madam, young man. It's luv round 'ere.'

'Would you like some raspberry jam?' I asked, thinking to do her a favour.

'Nay, lad, I makes me own!'

So said Mrs Robinson and so much for my salesmanship. She collected up her purchases and books and went off to the bacon counter to get her bacon ration from Bill Faulding.

A little while later came my turn for a coffee break so I left the counter to go upstairs to the staff room. As I drew near to the staff room door I could hear peels of laughter coming from inside the room. When I entered the laughter stopped abruptly and those present began to leave, looking rather sheepish as they went. Soon only Bill Faulding and I were left in the room and I asked him what all the mirth was about.

'Oh, nothing really, just a joke that someone had told,' he replied.

On my pressing him further, he reluctantly told me what it was all about.

'You remember serving a Mrs Robinson with her rations this morning?' he asked. 'Well, when she left you she came along to me for her bacon ration. "'Ere, Bill," she said. "Who's that new lad th' as got on't ration counter? Don't 'e talk lah-de-dah!" That's what I was telling them just before you came in,' said Bill Faulding.

It was at about this time that I had another 'skirmish' with Mother. I had just joined the Fulwood Church choir through my friendship with Cyril Norton who was a bass in that choir.

I have always enjoyed choral singing so it did not take much persuading for me to join. My mother got wind of this and rang me on the phone one evening:

'I hear you have joined the Church choir,' she said.

On my replying in the affirmative, she said,

'People of our strata do NOT sing in church choirs.'

I was both taken aback and rather angry at this attack on my harmless spare time activity, and replied,

'Well, they do now.' I replaced the phone. A poignant truce was maintained between us for quite a long time until she realized that I was not going to act on her obvious wishes.

14

Early in June after I had been at Castle Street branch for about three months and had had a spell in all departments including the confectionery bakery upstairs which supplied the shop and The Mikado cafe next door with all their requirements of fancy cakes, I arrived for work one morning and was told by the cashier, Mr Wilson, that Jimmy Barker had had a heart attack and would not be in to work for a while. This meant a telephone call to Head Office to the Managing Director as a result of which I was sent for to the telephone and told to take charge. In spite of my protestations that I had only been here a few months and that there were others more senior to me, I was told to get on with the job and not to argue. My new-found and exalted position was accepted by the staff and it was a case of business as usual though we were all very sorry to hear about Jimmy Barker — he was a popular and much respected manager, and very efficient at his job. Alas, he died a few weeks later.

A week or two earlier a new appointment to the head of the cooked meats counter had been made by Head Office and I had the feeling that all was not well in that department. After stocktaking at the end of September I received word that the results were far from satisfactory. This was the start of about two months of 'hell' for me for, try as we might, we could not get the results to improve. I was beginning to feel my inexperience as a shop manager but I had my suspicions regarding the person in charge of the cooked meats counter and these suspicions I voiced to the Managing Director at Head Office — to no avail. After three repeated stock-takes I became convinced that my suspicions were correct and a firm of investigators were engaged to try to find the source of the leakage. My suspicions were confirmed finally and I was told that I had the permission of the MD to sack the person concerned. This I did: an unpleasant job but a job in which I felt fully justified, bearing in mind the anguish I had suffered and the extra work put on the staff who had had to take stock every fortnight for the past two months. They carried out this extra work, without pay, most loyally and never complained — at least never to me!

We got through the winter all right and I recall vividly the time when the Sheffield Wednesday centre forward, Derek Dooley, had his leg broken one Saturday afternoon. It was a very hard winter — frosty and sharp — and the general air of calamity in the neighbourhood was most poignant. This area of Sheffield was composed of ardent supporters of 'Wednesday' and it was almost as though the country had suffered an international crisis of the first magnitude.

I got to know many of the local characters and stall holders in the market and many of the shop's customers became personal friends, especially Mrs Robinson, one of my very first customers who thought I spoke lah-de-dah! I remember one day a customer showed me a large roll of puce-pink ribbon which she had just bought as a bargain in the market. The ribbon was about one and a half inches wide and I had to agree it was a great bargain at two shillings.

'What are you going to use it for?' I asked.

'I don't rightly know but isn't it a good bargain!' she replied.

Amongst my numerous newly-made acquaintances was the manager of a wholesale firm of greengrocers in the market, and here in the following June I was offered some gorgeous-looking tomatoes straight from the grower in Lincolnshire. I took ten pounds in weight and they went like 'hot cakes'. They really were delicious and I wish I could remember their name. Anyway the next day a further consignment had come in and I offered to take the lot providing, of course, that the price was right. There were fifty trays — 600 pounds weight of tomatoes! I must be mad! However, the price was right and I was able to offer them for sale at a real low price and cleared the lot in a day and a half. I remember our storeman, Bert, coming to me and saying that there was a load of tomatoes for us and would I please come as there must be some mistake. There were far more than we could possibly handle. I went out to the van and I must confess I was inclined to agree with Bert. Fifty trays of tomatoes stacked in a van looks like one heck of a lot of tomatoes! The buyer at Head Office got to hear of this purchase of mine and words were exchanged but the deed was done and there was little he could do about it except pay the bill! The overall increase in the shop takings for that period vindicated my misdemeanour!

The manager of our main city centre store in Fargate, Mr Swift, was due to retire at the end of that September and, out of the blue, came a summons for me to present myself at Head Office because the Managing Director wished to see me. On arrival there I was sent up to the private office where I found both the Chairman, Mr Victor Bibby, and the Managing Director, Mr Charles Moss, awaiting my arrival. Trading conditions and prospects at Charles Street shop were discussed and they finally came to the point. I would be aware, of course, that Mr Swift was due to retire at the end of September and the position of manager at the main store at Fargate had been offered to Mr Thacker the manager of the two branches at Doncaster. Not surprisingly he had turned this offer down as he did not wish to leave Doncaster and therefore it had been decided to offer the post to me. It was not without some misgivings that they had decided on this appointment as there were many more senior men in the firm but they felt that it would be generally accepted amongst the rank and file. This attitude was, to my mind, one further example of the general antagonism towards the family. Anyway I accepted the post and it was agreed that I should start work at 38 Fargate on 1 October following. It was also agreed that the other half of the store (40 Fargate) comprising the bread, confectionery, tea and coffee, and the sweet counters should come under my command as well as the tea and coffee buying, blending and tasting, and the chocolate manufacturing department should also be peeled off from the cafe/restaurants and placed under the unified control of the store manager. Thus I became the manager of the whole of the Fargate store complex with control over the tea and coffee departments and the chocolate department at a salary of £1,000 per annum. This was a sensible arrangement in fact, as it was the shop that sold the goods concerned. Mr Albert Gregg was my right-hand man in the tea and coffee department. He had been associated with this side of the business for some years and his expertise was invaluable. It was not long before I received a further order from Head Office to go up to London for a week to learn

114

something about tea and coffee blending and buying so I spent a week with Messrs Appleton, Machin and Smiles who were our suppliers of these commodities. On my return Albert Gregg went up to Town on the same mission. On my taking over the management of the Fargate store, I had Mr Arthur Lent as my second-in-command and Mr Rollin as the cashier in charge of the order and cash office. Arthur Lent had been my father's platoon serjeant in the Green Howards after the first world war and on his retirement from the army my father had given him a letter of introduction to my grandfather for a post in the family business. Thus Arthur Lent had worked his way up to be assistant manager of the central retail store, as well as being a loyal friend to the Davy family. Mr Rollin, too, had been through the first world war and had been severely gassed. He, too, was a loyal and enthusiastic servant of the firm so I was very fortunate in having these two gentlemen in support.

One of the first things I did was to study the shop's weekly turnover and takings. Having got a picture in my mind I resolved to improve the situation, being quite sure that we must be missing out on trade. A little thought and study convinced me that we were lacking a delicatessen department but there were difficulties ahead as to where to site a new department. As luck would have it I came across an old refrigerated stainless steel table which I discovered had been used for such a purpose before the last war and which could be brought back into use. We polished it up and sited it near one of the entrance doors and started in a small way by establishing a specialist counter of cocktail accessories such as onions, cherries, cocktail sausages and the like. This was well received by our customers and I then asked the firm's Maintenance Department to fix the table up with refrigerant. After some difficulty this was done and I put Miss Lucy Bradley in charge with one young assistant to help her. Fresh salads were introduced, as well as cooked fresh salmon which was cooked for us in the restaurant kitchen, fresh York Hams on the Bone, smoked Ox Tongues — in fact anything of a delicatessen nature that commanded a demand and which was appropriate to that department. All these items had, of course, to be ordered direct from suppliers in London and it was not long before the inevitable happened — the chief buyer, Mr George Gaisford, started to complain that Mr Arthur (Davy) had taken upon himself to buy direct. This was contrary to the firm's policy of central buying but, as I pointed out when the matter was raised, the Fargate store was the only shop in the city where these items were stocked for sale and I was able to order them forward as and when I required them. The Powers That Be were still unconvinced so I was forced to play my Trump Card and threatened to close down the department which would mean a considerable loss of business. By this time early in 1952 the store takings had more than doubled and I was forced to add that if I was to be restricted in this way they could have my resignation. I won the day and we proceeded to further expand the takings and the profits, and trade blossomed.

A special effort was made for the Coronation period and as I had won my skirmish with the head buyer I decided to take a plunge when the representative from one of my suppliers called on me and offered an attractive lot of Cocktail Onions which his firm, Noels, were packing especially for the Coronation trade. These onions were packed in the same sized jar as their every day jar but they were attractively presented with three plastic cocktail sticks, in Red, White and Blue, affixed to the jar by means of a strip of Red, White and Blue sellotape. These were offered to me at a price which would enable me to put them on offer at two shillings and ten pence per jar as against the usual retail price of three shillings and six pence — a saving to the customer of eight pence per jar. This would be a really attractive proposition, I thought. On the strength of these terms I ordered Ten Gross (one thousand one hundred and forty jars!). Such is the fickleness of human nature that, when the onions arrived and I had put on a window and counter display, the sales were negligible — panic stations! I held a conference with Miss Bradley and Mr Lent and we removed ALL the jars from the display. I put two girls on to removing the cocktail sticks from the jars and then bunching these same sticks into bundles of six sticks which we secured with the self-same sellotape. We made out a special ticket, advertising the fact that they were on special offer at three pence per bundle! I asked for the printing department to make me some tickets showing these jars of Cocktail Onions as a special offer for the Coronation Only at the remarkably low price of three shillings and four pence. This was a return to the store of seven pence over the total which might have been obtained from the special price at which they were first on offer. We cleared the lot! I can only assume that the remarkably low price was viewed with suspicion by the local populace and that they assumed that these must be old stock! I was no less concerned myself but for a very different reason — I was in the midst of a duel with the head buyer, a form of truce had been declared after I had won my point that I should be allowed some latitude and it was imperative therefore that I should give him no cause to say 'I told you so.'

One further crisis occurred during my first year at the firm's premier store and that concerned the Easter window display. I have already mentioned that I had charge of the chocolate manufacturing department so I arranged with the manageress of the said department to let me have a collection of chocolate animals for a window display which I planned for the centre window of the store. I felt this to be both useful for prestige value as well as for sales promotion. All sorts of beautiful 'creatures' were made for me and I set to work with our window dresser to create a sensational window display for the Easter period. There was a chocolate rabbit about eighteen inches high together with three or four baby rabbits, a tortoise, a chicken, a lamb and some other animals. All these were laid out in the window display together with suitable background material and very well they looked too! For the first weekend the window was left with the lights switched on for the delight and, hopefully, the interest of the passing populace. That weekend the sun shone warmly upon Sheffield and at about eleven o'clock on the Sunday morning there was a telephone call for me at home from the police. Would I please come down to the store at once as the sun was melting the chocolate figures in the main window! Down to town I hurried and there before my eyes was the ghastly truth. The sun had indeed melted the chocolate figures and the bottom of the window was awash with a sea of liquid chocolate. All those beautiful figures were no more — disintegrated in the warmth of the sunshine! And the mess! . . . oh dear, oh dear! There was nothing for it but to lower the blinds over the window and leave the mess till Monday morning when I hoped the chocolate would have hardened and the mess easier to clear up. I suppose it was all my fault but I did so want to make a sensation. I did make the sensation all right but not in the way I had intended! The window was duly cleared out the next morning, a further display on a more modest scale was installed and Easter Week passed off without further mishap!

As the day for the Coronation of Her Majesty Queen Elizabeth II drew near it was decided that there was scope for the bakery and confectionery departments at the factory to cash in and a display of the coronation regalia was duly created and laid out in the centre window of the Fargate store. These were not real cakes but were made with all sorts of different materials for display purposes only. A notice was placed in the window inviting customers to order from the display and the real thing would be made to order in the factory. The staff on the confectionery counter was informed that these replicas were NOT for sale direct to the public as they were mock-up and not made of cake and/or icing sugar. At holiday and other busy times it was customary to engage some part-time staff and apparently the 'message' had not got through to them all. Imagine my horror therefore when I came back from my luncheon break and inspected the window as was my wont, to see a gap in the display where had stood the replica of the Coronation Orb. The price ticket was there all right but where was the Orb? Enquiries at the counter revealed that the orb had been sold but no one knew to whom it had been sold. No, it was not a regular customer so far as anyone knew. The part-time assistant had sold it to a customer who had been so insistent that she should have it there and then. The customer could not possibly wait for a special order to be placed for her so, rather than lose the sale, the assistant had sold the orb to her. Now, what should be done? Information was gleaned from the factory that this model of the orb had been made from a lavatory ball cock and sprayed all over with white icing to resemble the real thing. Any orders for this particular article would, of course, be made of rich fruit cake, coated with marzipan and icing. It was quite impossible to trace the customer concerned and it was not really the assistant's fault except that she had been over zealous. It was decided to place a carefully worded advertisement in the local paper, asking that the persons who had purchased a replica of the Coronation Orb from Davy's Fargate store should contact the manager. The store telephone number as well as my own private number was given and we awaited developments. Nothing happened at work but my wife reported that she had had a telephone call from one of the National dailies in London enquiring as to what had happened. They wanted to know if there was a story to be had — was poison involved?

Fortunately my wife, Mary, had the sense to know nothing about the matter although I had, naturally, told her all about it.

Coronation Day was fast approaching and on the Wednesday before the great day one of our van drivers reported seeing the Orb in the front window of a terraced house as he was passing. This news was duly passed to me and I set off at about four o'clock that evening to the address given to me. On arrival there I found myself outside a neat row of terraced houses and knocked at the front door. There in the front window was the Coronation Orb, placed in such a position for all to see — and very well it looked too! No answer. I knocked again — and again. Still no answer. The occupiers must be out at work and not yet returned. I left and went back again when we had shut up shop, at about six pm. This time I was in luck and a lady answered the door. I introduced myself and told her of my mission. I could not help but imagine the awful situation that would ensue if I failed to get the thing back — the moment of truth when a knife was plunged into the so-called cake and a metallic clang would ring out! The story would be all round the district and the name of Davy would be the laughing stock of the neighbourhood, quite apart from the possibility of litigation under the Misrepresentation of Goods Act. Whilst we were talking and I was not making very much headway a voice called out from the back room:

'What's the trouble, missus?'

Then the man of the house appeared. A big man in every respect. He seemed to tower above me and I am six feet tall, and he was built in like proportion. His wife explained to him the gist of the matter and I can recall the apprehension I felt as I watched his face. All this time his steely gaze never left me and I felt much as I had done at school when challenged by one of the staff over some misdemeanour. But I HAD to get back that Orb so I decided to come clean, and proceeded to explain what had happened. He listened intently to my explanation without giving any hint of his feelings and I began to fear the worst — he was going to make an issue out of this. I could almost hear him weighing up the amount of compensation he could get from the firm for selling an article which did not conform to reasonable standards. After a pause that seemed like hours he proceeded to point out to me that I, as the person responsible, had sold to a member of the public an article which was not of merchantable quality and, as a firm of food purveyors, had sold an article which was NOT fit for human consumption. How would this look in the local newspaper, he asked. I had to agree it would not look good and I also pointed out that it would not look good for the assistant who sold it. Suddenly when I was beginning to think that all was lost, he burst into peels of laughter, slapped me on the back and said:

'By gum lad, I reckon I had you worried there!'

He then asked me in for a cup of tea and we had an amicable discussion on the forthcoming Coronation and he told me of the party they had got planned and that the model of the Orb was to be the highlight of the festivities when he would cut into it at a moment yet to be decided. This sent him off into further paroxysms of mirth as he tried to explain his vision of the assembled company awaiting the great moment and the awful metallic clang as the knife struck the ball cock. The mention of the ball cock sent him off again and I must say the picture that he painted did seem rather funny and I had to join in the hilarity. But I still had NOT got hold of that Orb. We finished our tea and he suddenly got up from his chair, strode over to the window and picked up the offending article. Turning round he handed it to me and said:

'There ye are now. But let's be havin' the real cake ter morrer night 'cos t'neighbours'll be missin' it in t'winder.'

I promised I would be back with the real thing by the same time next day and departed with whatever dignity I had remaining. It was now getting late but I tracked down the bakery manager and begged him to have an Orb cake ready for me to take out the following evening. This he did and so ended one further episode in my experiences as a food store manager!

15

Soon after the date for the Coronation of Her Majesty The Queen was set, our regimental association held a draw for seats on The Mall to view the procession and, quite against the usual run of luck, I drew two seats. Mary was pregnant and medical advice was sought as to the wisdom of accepting this unexpected windfall. The baby was due on 10 June but, as our family doctor so rightly observed when we asked him whether or not we should risk the trip, Mary was early last time and he would advise against it. We took his advice and our second son was born on 4 June — as the Duke of Wellington is reputed to have remarked on another occasion 'it was a damned close run thing!' I am not a winner of raffles or lucky draws so it was fortunate that we turned down the opportunity or we might have joined the many others who had to leave their seats to be attended to by St John's ambulance staff!

The arrival of the new baby took place in the very early hours of 4 June and I was roused from my slumbers by the ringing of the telephone. It was our family doctor ringing to tell me that the baby boy had arrived and that mother and child were fine. He added that the baby looked remarkably like Mr Ernest (my paternal grandfather or Funny Grandad) and that if we kept up this form we would be heading for a cricket team. Nurse Mac had been engaged again as midwife and she came home with us as before to see to the child for the first two weeks. In other words the baby would be four weeks old when Mary assumed complete charge. How quickly those weeks went by! and how 'deaf' one became at night when the baby cried, wanting his feed or for whatever other reason babies have for crying!

At about this time I received a call from Messrs Pickford &

Co, from whom I had ordered a new car in 1947. I had even forgotten what sort of car I had ordered and it turned out to be a Hillman Minx Tourer. I had completely forgotten about this and, on top of the expense of a new baby, I was in a mind to cancel the order. However, my parents advised me to accept the car and they pointed out that I had been left 1,000 Preference Shares in Arthur Davy & Sons by my grandfather and that I could sell these shares to finance the purchase of the car. I had not considered this line but the more I thought about it, the more sensible it seemed to be. Anyway I had never owned a new car and now was the time to put that omission to rights. The price of a brand new Hillman Minx Tourer at that time in 1953 was just over £800 — when I ordered it in 1947 it was in the region of £750 so inflation was with us even then but not to the same extent as today. My stockbroker and cricketing friend, Mark Barber, arranged the sale for me and I received just over £800 for the shares which went straight into the purchase of my new car.

Whilst Mary was in the Nursing Home I became friendly with Mike Palmer, the elder brother of a school friend of mine. Mike's wife, also Mary, had given birth to a son so the two Dads agreed that we might look into the possibility of the two families joining forces and having a holiday together in September. We both employed 'au pair' girls so they could come as well and thus leave us parents free to enjoy a holiday. We were all sailing enthusiasts so Mike and I set off to West Wittering on the Sussex coast and found a very suitable farmhouse called Normanton Farm for letting at about twelve pounds per week which we accepted and reserved for the first two weeks in the following September. We also found a small sailing dinghy for charter at Bosham so we booked that as well and returned home well satisfied with our exploration. The holiday went off well and the two families remained friends in spite of it being said that the way to break a friendship is to go on holiday together!

At about this time Charles Moss decided to retire to Bournemouth and George Gaisford, the head buyer, took his place. George had been head buyer and had spent most of working life with the firm under my grandfather. It was with him that I had had my skirmishes as regards the buying of specialist items for the Fargate store's new delicatessen

122

department. It was the custom at this time for the Managing Director to call into the store after taking his luncheon in the restaurant, and George Gaisford carried on this routine. I was working very hard trying to beat the target figures set for the current year — with a fair degree of success I might add — when I was rung one day and told on the telephone by the MD that my salary was to be raised by fifty pounds per annum. I was somewhat taken aback by this information from the MD himself as the turnover at the store had all but doubled since I took over three years before. I took a deep breath and replied that if 'things' were as bad as that then perhaps it would be best if they were to keep it! There was a deathly hush the other end of the line and then the click of the receiver being replaced on its cradle.

'Oh dear,' I thought to myself, 'Now you've done it.'

George Gaisford came nowhere near me for the following few days and then, in the post from Head Office, came a type-written letter addressed to me personally.

'This is it. This is the sack,' I thought to myself.

But no, I was mistaken. Inside was an officially worded letter which ran as follows:

Dear Mr Davy,

It is with much pleasure that I have to inform you that at a recent meeting of the Board, the Directors have decided to increase your annual salary by £250 in recognition of the excellent results achieved at the Fargate Store under your management, over the past year.

With best wishes,

Yours truly,

(Sd) G.E. Gaisford

My father later told me that, whilst he was in full agreement with my sentiments, such a high-handed method of obtaining a salary increase was NOT to be recommended in the future!

16

The month of March 1954 saw the annual Peak District Point-to-Point Races and we all went out for the day. Mary's friend Annette Swan was staying with us at the time and my mother was trying to pull off a marriage between my sister, Eve, and Geoffrey Sandford with whom I was on friendly terms due to our mutual interest in cricket. We all arrived early at the course and Mary suggested we should walk the course before lunch. My mother and father declined the suggestion so the rest of us 'young people' set off for our walk. It was not long before Geoffrey and Annette paired off together whilst Eve remained with us. The racing over, we returned homewards and that evening just as we had gone to our beds came the first of the telephone calls. It was Mother. Four times she rang that night. The first two calls were answered by Mary as I was in my dressing room preparing for bed and the extension telephone instrument was in our bedroom. The third time I answered her call and she proceeded to tell me off for allowing Annette to go off with Geoffrey when he, Geoffrey, should have been paired off with Eve. In vain did I point out that I was NOT my sister's keeper nor could I be expected to arrange the pairing and anyway, what did she expect that I should have done about it? With that I rather abruptly put down the phone whereupon she rang back to say that I was a very rude 'boy' and very selfish and had no thought for my sister's happiness. An uneasy relationship developed between us for some days, so much so that Mary took a hand, saying that this was silly and then arranged a small dinner party to which she invited Eve and Geoffrey as the sole guests. Eve walked over to our house that night so that, after the evening was over, Geoffrey would be permitted to drive her home. This all went according to plan and a few weeks later they were engaged. Mother immediately became all sweetness and honey so one more family row was sorted out! Eve and Geoffrey were married in St John's church, Ranmoor the following November. The union with the Sandford family was considered eminently suitable as their name appeared on the Roll at Battle Abbey, as did that of my mother's family, Travers!

Our au pair girl was Irish. She came from a large family near Mountrath, in County Laois, and was of great value to us being both dependable and cheerful. She decided to stay with us for the Christmas 1954 and on Christmas Eve I invited her to have a drink with us. She refused on the grounds that she had 'taken the pledge', as was commonplace amongst her compatriots. I was a bit taken aback by this and more or less insisted that she should have a little drink in view of the fact that it was Christmas. I offered her a small Cherry Brandy.

'Oh, sure,' she said, ''tis only flavouring!'

On the strength of that I told her she should join us in the drawing room where she had a second drink. After that there was no holding her — fortunately the children had been put to bed!

In 1958 came the news that an offer had been made by Allied Bakeries to purchase the shares of the firm and that the offer had been accepted by the Directors. Allied Bakeries were the makers of Sunblest bread and they were expanding rapidly as supermarket owners throughout the country. They had had their eye on Arthur Davy & Sons since before the war and my late great uncle Arthur and Mr Garfield Weston, the chairman of Allied Bakeries were, so I was told, great friends. Prior to this development we ourselves had tried unsuccessfully to take over the local grocery firm of Burgons Ltd and we had also taken a half-hearted interest in Burtons of Nottingham but, as it appeared to me at the time, we did not have anyone of sufficient drive and business acumen to press home our case. Anyway here was a firm offer from a company of national repute to take over our business and the result was a foregone conclusion. Those of us in the family who were actually working in the firm together with those of our employees who had been given shares in the company over the years in recognition of their loyal service could muster only about five per cent of the total share holding. The remaining shares were held by various (mostly female) family members who were scattered around the world, mostly in Rhodesia, and who were not really interested in the livelihood of those of us who were working (for them) on the ground. Aunt Alice, Uncle Arthur's widow, still had a sizeable shareholding and was on the Board of Directors so there was no help to be counted on from those quarters — they wanted the money! A deal was struck and conducted for us by the chairman, Mr Victor Bibby, and we all received thirty shillings per ten shilling share. I was a real capitalist now and had £12,000 to invest. Riches beyond the dreams of avarice! And Mary had some too! A visit to my stockbroking friends was called for and an investment plan was drawn up. Thus, at the age of thirty-eight years I had become a stock exchange investor for the very first time! After the conclusion of the take-over I remember Aunt Alice telling me of the friendship between Uncle Arthur and Garfield Weston which friendship went back to pre-war days. It appeared that this friendship was based on their mutual interest in dry-fly fishing. She also added that if and when I was in London, she was sure that Mr Weston would be very pleased to see me if I were to call on him.

That autumn I received a circular from my old regimental association announcing that the Gurkha Brigade dinner would be held on a certain date in October and that His Royal Highness The Duke of Edinburgh was to be the guest of honour and would also be the guest speaker. I obtained leave of absence to attend the dinner and on the way up to town by train I resolved to call on the mysterious Mr Weston and thus find out for myself what sort of a tycoon it was for whom I was working. I presented myself at the enquiry desk of Fortnum and Mason and asked for Mr Weston, presenting my card at the same time. After a short interval a flunkey appeared and asked me to follow him, adding:

'Mr Weston will be pleased to see you now, Sir.' We ascended in the lift to the third floor where I was ushered into what appeared to be the Board Room and was duly announced:

'Mr Davy Mr Weston.'

In front of me was a GIGANTIC mahogany table with chairs arranged down either side and there, at the far end, sat Mr Weston himself. He rose from his seat and beckoned me to advance. With outstretched hand he bade me welcome with a:

'Come along and sit down, Mr Davy.'

126

I did as I was told and there followed a cordial and interesting conversation. He enquired about trade in Sheffield and told me about his friendship with Uncle Arthur which was based on their interest in fishing. He told me of his family interests in Canada and Australia, prompted no doubt by my telling him of my sister-in-law out in the Antipodes.

'You must let me know whenever you decide on a visit out there,' he said, to which I replied that I was not likely to go out there unless he sent me! After about an hour's chat he rang a bell and asked his secretary to bring a box of Harvest Gold biscuits which he said had just been perfected by one of his subsidiaries. I was to let him know what the reaction was amongst our shops' staffs.

* * *

The year also saw one of my more successful periods on the cricket field when I decided to go once more on the annual Devon Cricket Tour with the Sheffield Collegiate Cricket Club. The fixtures were the same as always but the 'lodgings' were different. Instead of staying at Sidmouth for the latter part of the tour, the team now stayed at a small country inn at Ottery St Mary near Exeter. The team was under the command of Philip Mountford and the spearhead of the attack was to be born by Ian Thompson. Alas, Ian 'broke down' during the second match so that when it came to the match against the Royal Naval College, Dartmouth, I was given the new ball to open the attack. I collected three wickets that day and well remember one of them in particular. I was bowling in-swingers as my main 'weapon' and having disposed of one of the openers I saw the next man, a Pakistani, coming in and having a word with the outgoing batsman. I could visualize the gist of the conversation — 'that fellow bowls in-swingers.' I sent down the remainder of the over as usual and after bowling one swinger to him at the start of my next over, I sent him a leg cutter. Just as I had hoped he played inside the ball, anticipating another in-swinger, and I bowled him off stump. People who deride the game of cricket, calling it dull and refusing to try to understand the finer points of the game cannot understand the satisfaction to be gained by tactics.

We moved on to the second part of the tour and I bagged

a couple of wickets against the Devon Dumplings at Exeter then the weather broke. It was blowing a gale when we arrived at the Exmouth ground and having lost the toss, we took the field. I was given the new ball to open the attack but so strong was the wind that I was quite unable to control the new ball which swung wildly off target. I was relieved to be taken off for a while until the shine was off the new ball. I was then brought back to bowl again and this time all was well. With the assistance of the strong wind blowing from the third man direction I was able to make the ball do just as I wanted and bagged five wickets which included my one and only hat trick. I followed this up by opening our innings and making quite a decent score and we won the match convincingly. The final match of the tour was against Sidmouth. I was so stiff after the previous day's exertions that I was quite unable to produce any sort of form at all and failed miserably with both ball and bat. So ended my last cricket tour with the Collegiate Cricket Club. One evening during the following winter John Biggin and his wife threw a party for the tour members at which I was presented with the ball on which is an inscription on a silver plaque listing the scalps which I secured at Exmouth. This is one of my treasured mementos and it sits on my desk to this day.

It will be remembered that at the time of my marriage to Mary I was unable to offer her a trip abroad for our honeymoon and that I promised her that we would go abroad within ten years. I found that in 1959 I was in a position financially to fulfil my promise and we booked a trip to Italy at the end of May. We flew to Rome where a hire car was awaiting us and thence motored to Ravello near Amalfi where we had booked in to the Hotel Caruso. The car was a Fiat 600 with a folding roof and we travelled overnight from Heathrow in a Vickers Viscount aircraft. This aeroplane was in its infancy and was considered to be the height of luxury. We left at three am and arrived in Rome at seven am — a total of four hours flying. At that time Mary did not drive so we made our way south in easy stages, arriving at our hotel just as dusk was falling. The hotel was a large, marble-interior building well run by Signor Caruso himself and providing every comfort for the visitor. The food was excellent and beautifully presented in a large, airy restaurant where the service was of the first order. Signor Caruso owned his vineyards and produced a very palatable house wine. As one ate one's evening dinner one could look down on the sea below and watch the fishing fleet with their little lamps at their mast heads, bobbing about on the water. These boats were after anchovies and went out each evening.

We had been warned before our departure that the Italians were very strict as to their decorum and that it was quite unheard of, for instance, for a lady to be seen in public with her shoulders bare. It was all right on the beach but one should NEVER be seen in public without one's shoulders covered. One day we were going down to Amalfi for a swim. As we were travelling in our little car we neither of us gave a thought to the rule about bare shoulders. Mary was wearing her newly-acquired sunsuit with bare shoulders but, as we were travelling in a car, we did not give a thought to the rule about dress. Just as we were leaving the village of Ravello we were sent on our way with a series of wolf whistles — Mary's bare shoulders had been spotted and greeted accordingly! What price present day behaviour, I wonder?

The sea water around Amalfi was FILTHY, and that was over thirty years ago. In those days the question of sanitation and pollution had not reared its head and vociferous minorities were unheard of. I wonder what the sea water at Amalfi is like today?

We spent about five days at Ravello and after the second evening we became conscious that two American tourists dining at the next table seemed anxious to make our acquaintance. We eventually met and they introduced themselves as Sam and Elinor Adler from Savannah in Georgia. We became good friends and went around a lot together. They were going on to Rome ahead of us and we arranged to meet them for luncheon at a well-known restaurant in the Via Venetzia on a specific day. This we did and ate cannelloni for which the restaurant was famous. I recall here a typically generous gesture on the part of Sam Adler. In those days we British were restricted in the amount of currency we could take out of the country. One could pay all one's travelling and hotel expenses in sterling before departure but one was allowed only twenty-five pounds in cash or travellers cheques to take on the trip. Sam, who was obviously a very wealthy man, expressed his amazement that we British were able to travel abroad at all. He put his hand in his pocket, pulled out a roll of ten dollar bills, handed them to me on the table and said:

'Here you are — enjoy yourselves. I cannot think how you people can possibly get along on your meagre allowance.'

This was a truly embarrassing moment and I said:

'It's very kind of you, Sam, but we couldn't possibly accept this,' and pushed the money back towards him, hoping not to appear ungrateful.

He pushed the roll of notes back towards me and said:

'Go on, take them. We are visiting London after a few days in Paris and you can pay me back then.'

Little did he know the state of my bank balance. If he did, he would not have said that! I managed to dissuade him and assured him that we could manage and we were thus able to remain as friends. During the course of our last day in Rome I found a parking ticket affixed to the windscreen of the car for One thousand lire. Needless to say I did not pay this fine and duly returned the car to the hirers before our departure that same evening. I suppose my name still appears on Italian police files as an undesirable alien or maybe my 'crime' is still on their books as unsolved!

Whilst in Rome we became caught up in the Whitsun festivities. We were visiting the Colosseum at the time and noticed a crowd of people gathering on the roads round and about. On enquiring what it was all about we were told that the Pope was due to pass by at noon to be present at a service to be held at the Triumphal Arch. We could see this arch from where we stood so we decided to stay and witness this spectacle. This we did and were curious to notice that during the service of Corpus Christi which one could assume was a holy and reverend occasion, everyone around us was chattering and smoking as if nothing was happening at all! Apparently they had only turned out for something to do and the service was of little consequence. How very odd, we thought!

We went to the opera one night to see *Mephistophles*. Mary had a sleeveless evening dress and, as we had experienced before, in those days it was not done for ladies to appear in public with their shoulders uncovered so a special sortie had to be made to purchase a shawl to wear that evening.

When the time came for our departure we arrived at the airport to be told that our flight to London was delayed and that take off would not happen until about three am. We wandered about for some time and eventually found ourselves in a small cafe/bar somewhere near the airport where a few people were gathered. It was here that we were introduced to an Italian liqueur called *Strega* — a very pleasant and moreish beverage. We also got talking to an Italian who was a courier for Thomas Cook, the travel agents, and who was also waiting for the same flight to London as ourselves.

On the return flight we crossed over the Alps just as dawn was breaking and I was able to take some impressive ciné photographs of the mountains as we passed over them, including a particularly good view of Mont Blanc. We were flying in a Vickers Viscount again at about 20,000 feet and in those days to be able to view and to photograph the Alps was quite a talking point — in fact we did dine out on the experience for many weeks afterwards!

We returned home to Sheffield by train and I do recall the first time I got the car out and set off to collect one of our children. Mary shouted at me:

'You are on the wrong side of the road!'

Such are the habits of a lifetime broken by a short interlude in a foreign land!

That autumn I handed in my notice to leave the firm at the end of the year having secured a job at Westbourne Preparatory School in Sheffield. I was to be head of the French department which took boys of twelve to fourteen years of age through Common Entrance and/or scholarship for entry to the public school of their choice. I had to accept the salary much lower than the salary I was now receiving from Arthur Davy & Sons — exactly half in fact — but I anticipated being much happier, and as a consequence much easier to live with! George Gaisford told me I could leave a week before Christmas so I took leave of the old family firm and prepared for the new job ahead. To prepare myself for this change of career I enrolled in night school for a term to brush up on my French which had become very rusty over the years of neglect. Early in the New Year I was invited to attend a farewell gathering in Victoria Cafe, Fargate where nearly all the shops managers and other heads of departments were assembled. To my surprise and delight I was presented with a gold wrist watch, inscribed on the back with these words: 'Presented to A.E. Davy from his colleagues in Arthur Davy & Sons Ltd. December 1959.' The Managing

Director, George Gaisford, made a little speech of farewell and good wishes and one particular phrase stands out in my memory. It ran as follows: 'I wish to stress that Mr Arthur leaves the firm entirely of his own free will.'

What a strange thing to say, I thought, but then again there was a certain amount of uncertainty and unrest prevalent amongst the workforce at that time. I knew this from my contacts and visits to the branches during the previous few months. The meeting passed off with words of goodwill and good wishes on all sides and thus I severed my connections with the family firm — a company which had sustained the Davy family for almost a hundred years and was now in the ownership of outsiders. The centenary was due to fall in 1967 and I wondered if anyone would even know about it.

17

I started work at Westbourne Preparatory School, Sheffield on 21 January 1960 where I took over the teaching of French to boys in the fourth, fifth and two sixth forms (6a and 6b). The boys in 6a were the scholarship candidates and many of them were as well versed in the French language as I was! I did find that the few weeks I had spent on a French course at evening class were beneficial to me as I was able to polish up on pronunciation and grammar which had become somewhat rusty after so many years lying dormant. I soon settled into the swing of things and enjoyed the new life which at last seemed to have a purpose. I was Form Master of the fifth form (eleven to twelve year olds) and as it was the Easter term we had to produce a play towards the end of term. We chose two episodes from *Alice in Wonderland*, namely The Mad Hatter's Tea Party and the trial scene based on Tenniel's famous picture for which we received applause from the audience when the curtain went up. I must say those of the staff who were responsible for make-up did a magnificent job and the effect was most striking. The following two terms were uneventful and I was happily settled in my new way of life. I believe Mary was much happier too and, of course, I got the two boys educated free into the bargain! In the summer term I was put in charge of junior cricket and was able myself to resume playing for Sheffield Collegiate Cricket Club on a Saturday afternoon and was promptly appointed as Captain of the 'A' team. We had a very good season and never lost a match — those that we did not win we drew!

Whilst on the subject of cricket I was selected one Saturday to play in the Yorkshire Council team against Maltby. This was a colliery town and they fielded a proficient cricket team which was well supported by the local populace. Whilst fielding deep on the boundary a colossal hit from an opposing batsman came my way. It soared up into the air and as I placed myself to take the catch, a voice could be heard amongst the crowd:

''E'll drop it, tha' knows. Mark my words, 'e'll drop it.'

I did, in fact, catch it and the crowd were the first to express their approval!

I did incur the wrath of the Headmaster on one occasion when on one Saturday morning when the senior boys came in for extra tuition I was heard chatting to my class all about golf and cricket when we should have been involved in a French lesson! This happened because there was a grammatical point about the translation of the word 'play' into French and I fear I got side-tracked by the pupils: something we all have attempted to do in our younger days! Come the following spring term, the Headmaster decided to put on a Gilbert & Sullivan comic opera and he chose *HMS Pinafore*. This released us form-masters from having to put on a play ourselves and the school performance went off very well. Whilst on the teaching staff at this school I was persuaded into taking up golf and four of us used to go off together for a round at Renishaw, a club not far from Sheffield. I enjoyed golf though I never attained a great degree of proficiency at the game — a good excuse for a walk!

During the summer holidays we went to stay with my parents who had, at the time of the take-over of the family firm, retired to Burley in Hampshire. Whilst we were there we visited Philip and Pat Deane in Dorchester. Philip used to be the mathematics teacher at Westbourne Preparatory School and about two years previously they had invested in a small preparatory school in Dorchester called Sunninghill, situated in Herringston Road. The school consisted of about seventy-five pupils and took boys and girls up to the Eleven Plus examination. Philip told us it was his intention to develop the school into an all-boys preparatory school with boarding facilities. We were persuaded into joining them in a partnership and to open the boarding house if a suitable house could be found nearby. We did find such a house further down Herringston Road called Ashford at number fifteen, so Mary and I joined Philip and Pat in their enterprise in the Easter term 1962. It was decided to form a limited company so in addition to the purchase of the house we also had to buy our fifty shares and also half the assets of the school, amounting to some £5,000 all told. Amongst the various reasons for our move down south was the fact that my father had developed Menier's disease which was affecting his balance and it was good to feel that we were close at hand in case anything should happen to him. We had also had enough of the Sheffield winters and we hoped that by moving south we would gain some relief from the hard winters. Little did we know! We left Sheffield and Westbourne Prep School at the end of the Christmas term and set off immediately for Dorchester, breaking our journey for the night at Warwick. We ran into thick fog later in the afternoon and had the unnerving experience of meeting a double-decker bus coming towards us on a one-way road — we were right and he was wrong! We arrived in Dorchester the following morning and awaited the arrival of the removers who quickly had our goods and chattels into the house. It was bitterly cold and all the water pipes were frozen solid! Anyway that did not matter as we were spending Christmas with my parents in Burley so we just set off there and then and left everything until after the festive season was over. On our return all pipes were still frozen so the plumber had to be sent for to unfreeze us — a somewhat inauspicious start to our new life.

Before the start of the Easter term there were certain formalities to be attended to in regard to our integration into the school. It had been decided that we should operate as a limited company so we had to have business sessions with the lawyers, pay over our agreed monies and so on. It was not until some time later that I began to realize that we were being 'used'. Our fellow directors were deeply in debt to the bank, their prospects of changing the school from an Eleven Plus day school for girls and little boys into a real preparatory school for boys only, with boarding facilities were tenuous in the extreme. We were quite successful in our academic endeavours and managed to obtain an above-average number of passes both into the local grammar school and also into Sherbourne School for Girls but I discovered very early on that discipline was very lax. I felt then, and I still feel now, that a 'benevolent' dictatorship, especially in schools, is both reassuring to the pupils and also to the staff. The 'human animal' performs much more readily when he or she knows the rules and is prepared to stick to them. There was one other male member of staff. He was not a particularly good teacher and his discipline in class was obviously poor. Philip was all for sacking him in favour of a retired army officer and I, to my shame agreed. Whilst I do not think we made an error in disposing of one of our staff, his replacement was not a good thing.

We were approached one day by a gentleman, a scientist at the nearby nuclear plant at Winfrith named Mr Hussein who wanted us to take his son who was at that time attending a state primary school. He wanted his son to go on to All Hallows School, near Lyme Regis and this meant that the boy had to pass the Common Entrance examination. The boy was then twelve years of age and this was a challenge we both appreciated. We asked if we could see the boy and assess the possibility of his passing the examination. Philip assessed him for Mathematics and I did the same for English. He had studied neither Latin nor French so there was no point in trying to assess his potential in either of these subjects. We both agreed that he was a very intelligent lad and that, within the year, we should be able to attain the required standard with him. We took him on and did not regret our decision for he passed the Common Entrance examination with flying colours. It was a pity in some ways that we did not have him much earlier on as it is highly likely that he would have gained a scholarship, thus saving his parents a great deal of money!

After our first term we were ready to accept boarders and in the summer term we had four boys boarding with us. The most we were able to muster was six and that was only because the winter weather was so harsh that we were asked to take two or three others to save the parents from having to make the hazardous journeys in to school each day! This was obviously 'not on' so, realizing my mistake in joining forces with the Deanes, I looked around for another appointment and was fortunate enough to be offered a post at Forres School, near Swanage as an assistant master. I did feel at the time that this was rather a tough school for small boys but 'any port in a storm' and they did offer us some accommodation in the form of a small bungalow. One thing I did not like the sound of was having to be up at seven am to take P.E.! When next I met Philip I was horrified to learn that he proposed to leave Sunninghill at the end of the summer to take over the headship of Clayesmore Preparatory School — an old established prep school for boys which sent most of their pupils to Clayesmore Public School. This development put us in a difficult position as it meant that the two of us would be leaving Sunninghill at the same time. Philip indicated to me that he would prefer to be in a real prep school for boys, preferably with full boarding facilities, so there was no question of him changing his mind — it was therefore up to us. I did not like the idea of letting down the parents or their children who were relying on my commitment to Forres School but, after much heart-searching I wrote to the Headmaster at Forres School and asked to be relieved from my commitment to join his staff. The HM was very understanding and, in spite of the fact that my request must have put him to a great deal of inconvenience, he wrote back immediately to say he quite understood my dilemma and would grant my request. Our traumas then really began. The Deanes wrote to all parents to tell them of their decision to leave but, at that time, we ourselves had not got clearance from Forres School. Notices of withdrawal of pupils came pouring in by every post and by the time we were able to announce our intention of carrying on, the numbers on the school roll of pupils had dropped from seventy-two to forty-four, and that was the number with which we started our first term. We did not dispense with any of the staff and just hoped for the best. By the Christmas term 1965 our pupil numbers had risen to sixty-eight and when we left the school in 1966 we had reached a total of eighty-two. This figure of eighty-two was, in fact, just over our target figure of eighty which we had set ourselves! The amount of work was intense and the strain had taken its toll. I must here pay a warm tribute to my wife, Mary, who acted as a filter between me and the parents. All sorts of problems manifested themselves and we were constantly in the firing line to act as mediators in family feuds and domestic quarrels. Anyway we got by and the parents seemed satisfied with our stewardship.

In 1965 my uncle Petrie Watson died so I became entitled to my share of Aunt Elsie's estate. We therefore bought a house in the neighbouring village of Cerne Abbas and were thus able to vacate our private quarters in the school building. This move proved a boon to our general health and well-being as we were able to leave our work behind us at the end of each day and so we became commuters! Although I did not realize it at the time, the workload on both of us was quite considerable. Mary was able to stay at home on some days in the week but I was not able to indulge myself in this luxury. The time came when

I felt I should quit the job. I know myself to be over-conscientious and I found the business of coping with the children as well as their parents was making me irritable and in consequence my teaching was suffering. The final straw came when my back which was always inclined to be troublesome, finally gave way and I was forced to face up to reality and to find a successor. We were fortunate here and I was able to hand over a thriving concern to Mr Purgavie who, strangely enough, had been an assistant master at Winchester Lodge in Torquay, the school where I had had my first job under George Butler. Mr Purgavie held a B.Sc degree and was able to take over without too much trouble.

And so we retired, or had we? On being relieved of the responsibilities of headmaster we took ourselves off to Teneriffe for a fourteen-day holiday, staying at the Hotel Neptuno. This was in the early days of package holidays so the island was not too crowded but there were a number of Germans in the hotel and they did get down early to the swimming pool to 'bag' the poolside seats! We flew out there in a VC10 of British Overseas Airways. This was (and I believe still is) a magnificent aircraft. As we were leaving the African coastline the captain came on the intercom to tell us that we would soon be making our descent to the island of Gran Canaria but that we had to maintain our height until the last possible moment as we were crossing the main air routes from East to West. Looking out from the windows we could JUST see the island 35,000 feet below. It resembled a postage stamp and we wondered how on earth we could possibly land on that! Once more the same voice came over the intercom.

'Please fasten your seat belts — we are about to make a vertical descent. Not to worry!'

A few seconds later the aircraft seemed to tip onto its nose and we were indeed making a vertical descent. The feeling was similar to that experienced when going downhill in a coach and one could feel the airbrakes holding back the plane. We levelled out a few thousand feet above the sea and came in to land at Gran Canaria in a perfectly normal way. After customs formalities we transferred to a smaller aircraft for a short flight across to the neighbouring island of Teneriffe. We were intrigued by this service. After all the passengers were aboard, the pilot came across the tarmac accompanied by two casually dressed gentlemen. He climbed aboard and they all continued their conversation — the pilot from his seat in the aircraft and his two companions on the tarmac. I have no idea of the substance of their conversation but whatever it was entailed much gesticulating and raised voices.

The time came for departure and the pilot proceeded to start the two Pratt and Whitney engines. One engine refused to fire! The two men on the ground were then co-opted to investigate and all was subsequently put to rights. The engine fired and we were off! I still wonder whether the two strange men were in fact aero engineers who were present in anticipation of trouble with that one engine! Anyway we made it and were soon transported aboard a Volkswagon minibus to the Hotel Neptuno, situated on the north west corner of the island.

Whilst sole headmaster of Sunninghill school I was invited to join the Rotarians and John Tynegate and I became the newest recruits to that august body which does so much good for local charities.

18

The Hotel Neptuno was a newly constructed and commissioned hotel and the restaurant was situated some distance away from the main hotel complex. The food was good and the hotel was quite comfortable. It had its own swimming pool, filled with sea water pumped up from the sea below and the beach was reached down a rough scree of several hundred feet. The beach itself was of rough volcanic rock and gravel and was not conducive to picnicking or bathing. Unfortunately the sea water pump was out of action so the water in the swimming pool was of a murky green colour and had obviously not been changed for some considerable time. There were many German guests in the hotel and, as usual, they would 'bag' the poolside chairs before breakfast by putting their towels etc thereon. We who were not members of the 'master race' were content to take a back seat, but one of our Anglo-Saxon number decided that the Hun should be taught a lesson to share the good life. He would do the rounds of the reclining chairs after the Germans had done their rounds and he would mix up the towels etc and occasionally spray the articles with water as though the gardeners had been busy with their hose pipes hosing down the swimming pool surrounds and plant pots! This caused some consternation amongst the victims, as was the intention, but we 'inferior beings' did get a look in!

Whilst staying at the Hotel Neptuno we struck up a 'rapport' with the Head Porter who was courting an English girl working in the neighbouring village. One day they shared a taxi with us for a trip up Monte Teide, an extinct volcano of some 7,000 feet in height in the centre of the island. All the islands which form the Canary Islands are volcanic and Monte Teide was the centre of volcanic activity until all such activity ceased many centuries ago. I had formed a desire to ascend this mountain ever since reading a travel article in the *Sunday Express* in which was described in some detail the splendours of the ascent of the mountain and the lunar-like landscape once one had left the vegetation behind. Also it was possible, so it was written in the article, to find a wild violet-like flower growing amidst the arid and desolate landscape. Quite true. We did, in fact, find these mountain violets growing coyly and in scattered isolation in a featureless desert, living entirely on moisture from the air or so it seemed, for there was certainly no nourishment to be gained from the lava-like terrain in which they grew. It was bitterly cold up there and the air was damp and forbidding in spite of the brilliant sunshine. The effect was most impressive and, indeed, sinister as one looked down onto a blanket of thick, rolling cloud which completely obliterated the landscape below. The silence was almost intolerable. There was no living soul in sight and the only sound was the low soughing of the incessant wind which chilled us through and through. As we were driven down the mountain side the sun shone into the back window of the car and one could feel the burning effect on one's shoulders, so much so that it became essential to cover them with a cardigan or some such garment to guard against severe sunburn. Even so, the sun's rays penetrated the covering and Mary suffered a mild sunburn through her cardigan. I was more fortunate as the sun's rays were unable to penetrate through my sports jacket. Our friend the Head Porter told us that Generalissimo Franco had planned the invasion of the Spanish mainland whilst in the Canary Islands and that his name was taboo amongst the local islanders. We had been warned!

On our return to England I took up a part time post as English teacher in the junior house at Hardye's Grammar School in Dorchester. I had been approached by the then Headmaster of the grammar school whose daughter had been a pupil of ours at our preparatory school, and I had agreed to join his teaching staff on a part time basis which was to cover three days a week from eleven am to four pm. I felt this would be an interesting appointment as there were a number of our own past pupils from Sunninghill who had moved on to the Grammar school via the eleven-plus examination and it would be good to see them again and to see how they were progressing. The salary was very basic as I did not hold a teaching diploma but what I did

NOT bargain for were the strict lines of demarcation which prevailed amongst the staff. I was to be rudely awakened in this respect before I had been there very long!

When I reported for duty at the start of the summer term 1966 I found that the three classes I had to teach were a very mixed bag, coming as they did from a variety of backgrounds. There were the sons of farmers, shop keepers, lawyers, scientists, doctors and many others and they had come to the grammar school through the eleven-plus examination from a wide range of different primary schools. Some, like our own past pupils, had come from fee-paying preparatory schools and others were from State-run primary schools with all sorts of backgrounds, catchment areas and the like. The average size of the classes was about twenty-eight to thirty boys so that one had a wide range of personalities with which to deal. Some children 'tried it on' to gain attention, some 'tried it on' to establish themselves as leaders of the pack. Some were studious, others were not, whilst some were nothing more than a nuisance — and one was led to wonder how they had managed to get through the system at all. Corporal punishment, administered only by the headmaster and witnessed by a member of staff, was still permitted in those days though the anti-corporal punishment lobby was becoming vociferous and gaining ground rapidly. I had to witness two canings but I cannot recall what were the offences. During my first term I got into trouble with the staff myself. It must be remembered that I had come from the private sector where (dare I say this?) one taught for the love of it and at a salary which was, in those days, much below the salary applicable to the job in the state system. However, it was and still remains my maxim that job satisfaction and fulfilment are of more importance than the remuneration. A minimum wage is of course, vital but nowadays it would seem to matter little so long as the salary is good. 'Keep up with the Joneses and the Devil take the hindermost' seems to be the norm today and I fear that Trade Unionism has a lot to answer for in this respect. The Union General Secretary has to justify his high salary, of course!

To return to my story. The misdemeanour which, incidentally, will go some way towards bearing out the gist of my quarrel with work attitude, was in this guise. During the post-lunch break I was on duty in the playground and one of my past pupils from Sunninghill days asked me if I would take a cricket net after school that evening. Three or four of his friends would be present but it was not an official practice evening. I was quite used to such a request and readily agreed. We would forgather at the nets at four fifteen pm and be finished by six pm in time for the boys to catch the bus home. Each boy had a 'knock' and we were off and away by five forty-five pm. Two days later I was summoned to the headmaster. He came straight to the point:

'Since when have you been appointed Games Master?' he asked. This was a line of questioning I least expected and I was at a loss for an answer. Finally I pulled myself together and realized that someone had 'split' on me regarding Tuesday evening's net practice.

'I am not the Games Master,' I replied, wondering what was coming next.

'Oh, really,' he said. 'I hear you were taking a cricket net last Tuesday. Is that right?'

'Yes,' I replied, 'Young Smith asked me to take a net as he and three pals would like a practice.'

'Oh, is that so,' said the head. 'Did it not occur to you that it was none of your business to be instructing in cricket?'

'No,' I retorted. 'So far as I am concerned it was out of school hours and I was free to please myself. Anyway I am a keen cricketer and am always happy to join in if anyone wants to play.'

'Well,' he said, 'let me tell you that Mr Bradshaw is very upset about it and I think an apology is due to him. Please remember in future that we all have a job to do here. Your job is to teach English and not to meddle with games or sport. If any help is required in this regard you will be approached by the member of staff in charge of games. Is that quite clear?'

Suitably chastened I withdrew. I had heard of the closed shop and demarcation but this was something I had not forseen and, to my uninitiated mind was quite ridiculous. No wonder the State Education system was in difficulties and so I began to wonder whether I had done the right thing in taking this job. Perhaps I and 'The System' were not compatible. Maybe I was, and still am, out of step with present-day thinking but, unless one is deliberately causing distress or hardship I do feel that life is for living and that one should be left to get on with it provided one does not disobey the law, of course. The foregoing incident was soon forgotten and I continued with my job as a teacher until the next incident occurred which finally decided me that I was not cut out by temperament for this kind of life.

As was the practice in my previous appointments it was useful to make preparations for the following lesson by putting something on the blackboard, thereby saving time. Towards the end of breaktime one day I was on my way upstairs when I met the assistant headmaster on the stairway.

'Where are you going?' he asked.

'I'm just going to 4B to prepare for the next lesson. It will save a bit of time if I put a few items on the blackboard for them.'

He glanced at his wristwatch.

'The next lesson does not start for another ten minutes. You'd best go back to the staff room.'

There was no doubt but that this was an order and that I had once again transgressed the 'rules', so I retraced my steps to the Common Room as instructed, vowing that enough was enough and that I had best find another job. I wrote out my notice that night after talking the situation over with Mary, and handed it in the next morning — the date was 8 June 1967, just before half term.

Early in the same year my elder son, Patrick, informed us that he wanted to go in for agriculture. We had been enquiring around as to the price of land in Dorset, Wiltshire and Devonshire and had decided that £200 per acre was awfully dear! As Mary was the sister of a well-to-do Irish farmer in County Cork we decided to explore the possibilities in Ireland. As luck would have it we had spent two weeks of our holiday in the previous year doing a care-taking job for the Scotts whilst they were away on their continental holiday. This had given us an insight as to whether or no we should like a life on the land. All had gone well and I was able to amuse myself by spraying the barley crop, and the two of us would wander around the farm to keep the men up to the mark as the sugar beet crop had to be thinned during our stewardship.

I enjoyed my fortnight as a farmer, I have always been a country lover and our spell at The Glen confirmed me in my desire to return to the country life which the war had interrupted. Imagine my joy therefore when Patrick made his decision to go in for agriculture. He had been a source of worry to his mother and to me for some years as he did not appear to have any particular preference for a career. He seemed to be a drifter. Now, at last, he had made a statement as to his future. He had collected a few passes in his 'O' levels and GSE examination at the age of seventeen years and as there did not appear to be any future examination successes in the offing I started looking for a suitable farm for us. His younger brother, Richard, had just started at All Hallows School, near Lyme Regis and was not involved in the scheme of things at this juncture.

It soon became apparent that land in south west England was far too expensive for us and so we turned our attention to Ireland. After all, my wife was Irish born and bred and her brother had inherited the family farm down in County Cork so the draw to Southern Ireland was obvious. Various Estate Agents were contacted and circles were drawn on a map of the country in an endeavour to find a property within about fifty miles of a port of exit and access so that our children's education would not be interrupted. Patrick had still one more year to complete.

Estate Agents are a strange breed! We approached three firms initially in our search for a suitable farm — in counties Cork, Wexford and Wicklow and the resulting response was both interesting and infuriating! We had stipulated that we wanted a house of not more than four bedrooms on approximately 100-150 acres of land suitable for mixed farming of cattle and tillage, well watered and fenced and within about fifty miles of Cork City, Rosslare or Dublin, and within easy reach of a livestock mart. We were sent sheafs of details about small estates, large houses of seven to eight bedrooms with stabling for twelve or more horses, forty acre parklands and so forth and, in consequence, we spent a lot of money and time in travelling to and fro to view these properties. It was whilst on one of these jaunts that we dropped on Ballyknockan, near Rathdrum in county Wicklow which property eventually became our home and farm. We were staying at The Glen in County Cork at the time as we were over in Ireland to view what seemed to be a likely property in County Wicklow. This turned out to be a newly-built two storey house in the middle of a field. There was no water laid on in any of the fields which had to be serviced with a water trailer every day. There were no hedges or trees or woodland of any kind and thus there was no shelter for animals and the approach to the house was by way of a dirt track across a field. Not for us, thank you!

We had brought Mary's brother Ted with us and we spent the night at the Grand Hotel in Wicklow Town where we met up with a Mr Dennis Collins who was the Department of Agriculture milk tester for the district. Dennis Collins hailed from County Cork and made his base at the Grand Hotel whilst doing his work around the county and would go back home to County Cork at weekends.

The following morning as we prepared to retrace our steps homeward to The Glen we called at the estate agent's office in Wicklow Town to tell them that we did not like what we had been to see. It was pouring rain and we were told that a property had just come on the market that very morning, that the agent (Harry Delehunt) knew the property and the vendor, and he would personally pilot us out there. The property was a short distance from Rathdrum and he felt it would suit us admirably as it fulfilled all the criteria we had laid down. Mary and I demurred but Ted persuaded us to go and have a look at it. He pointed out that we were in the district and it MIGHT be just right. The house was approached from the country road down a rough-surfaced, unfenced avenue about 350 yards long. This avenue led past the turn-off to the farm yard which was some seventy-five yards from the residence. The bungalow residence was built in 1946/47 and presented the appearance of being uncared for. The front was muddy and unsurfaced; the paintwork, in marian blue, was peeling off the metal window frames and, on our arrival which was unannounced, children issued forth from all direction. There were seven of them and Mary refused to leave the car!

'I'm not going in there,' she said. 'Look at the place! It's like something I've never seen before nor want to see again!'

She gave a further look at the bungalow and I must confess that I rather agreed with her. The bungalow looked 'down at heel', the paintwork was peeling and the roof was of cedar shingles which had obviously been there since the bungalow was built some twenty years before. There about 2,000 Christmas Trees planted on the front lawn and she felt that she could not cope with such a mess. Ted thought otherwise!

'It's the land that matters,' said Ted. 'You can work on the house at your leisure.'

With that profound statement he got out of the car and went round to the rear to fetch the spade from the boot.

We were now surrounded by the Flannery family and were invited into the house for coffee. There was no carpet on the sitting room floor, just a rug or two, and Ted and I left to walk round the farm. The land sloped towards the south and was bounded on the southern side by the river Avon. The fields down there were let on conacre (a letting for eleven months) to a local farmer-cum-contractor and were under a crop of barley. The land seemed in good heart. The northern part of the farm on which the owner's cows were grazing was about forty acres in area. There was no water and the only water supply for the whole property came from a surface spring about fifty yards from the house, from which a pump and pressure tank supplied water to both the house and yard. The asking price was £18,000 or some £137 per acre! The entire proposition seemed attractive so we left — to think about it.

It was 17 June.

Before returning to the UK and on our way home via Dun Laoghaire and Holyhead, we paid a return visit to Ballyknockan. The place still attracted us although it was in a very rundown state. A considerable sum of money would have to be spent on capital projects such as boundary fencing and water supply so, after our return to Cerne Abbas I rang the agent and made an offer of £12,000! This was turned down straight away as I anticipated so I made my supplementary offer of £14,000. Harry Delahunt promised to approach the vendor and ring me back the next day which he did. Flannery would accept £16,000 and we finally closed the deal at £15,500 or £118 per acre. I felt we had done quite well in view of the going rate of land in south west England and we moved there in the month of September, having previously arranged for the delivery of 200 bales of straw and also for a local builder, Vincent Holt, to install a fireplace and chimney in the sitting room together with a picture window and a small extension with access to the garden from the sitting room. These alterations were to be completed by the time of our arrival to take up residence on 22 September. Larry Flannery was to leave for our use his ancient Fordson TVO Tractor complete with trailer. This was to prove very useful to us for drawing in straw bales from the lower fields which bales we had purchased from Liam Clarke, the local farmer-cum-contractor.

147

Flannery also left a diesel-engine-driven corn mill complete with Lister diesel engine which he said he would arrange to collect at a later date. Meanwhile we were at liberty to use it.

On our return to the UK I thought it right and proper to tell my parents about our purchase of a farm in Ireland and of our impending departure to that country. Mother and father were visiting Eve in Sheffield at the time of our return so I wrote to them at home, to await their return. I was more than a little upset to receive a reply from my father couched in rather bitter terms and this is an extract from his reply:

21 July '67

'. . . Your hasty action at deciding to move to the Free State so quickly has hurt your mother and me more than I can say. We knew you were ultimately going there and the best of luck to you over it, but we did not bargain for quite such a hurried exit. We have had more than a year of intense anxiety over Eve which is not ended yet and it was always a comfort to us to feel you were within easy reach in an emergency.

It certainly looks at having taken the last penny you can get out of us, you turn your back on us and finis! We have not made these Trusts and Gifts without making some sacrifice to ourselves . . . .

Having been through the mill ourselves, your mother and I have always tried to co-operate and make things as smooth as possible for you within our limits and I can only hope that your capital is now not going to be frittered away in your last and most hazardous undertaking.

Your affectionate Dad.'

The receipt of this letter caused me a lot of hurt and I let a few days pass before I replied as follows:

'My dear Dad,

I have received your letter and noted the contents. I am indeed sorry you have felt obliged to react in this way as I should have thought you would know that the last thing I like to do is to cause hurt to anyone no matter what may be done to me.

148

*I have always tried, perhaps too much, to string along with
the family and have never at any time entertained such cruel
thoughts as you suggest about "taking every penny I can get
and turning my back and 'finis'." However, I must receive
your bitter judgement on my action which is prompted solely
by a desire to do the best for my end of the family within
the limits I have set for ourselves and as circumstances
dictate . . . .*

*I can now only hope that you and Mum will come to accept
that we have a life to lead too, that we are not departing to
the ends of the earth and that I still remain*

Your loving and affectionate son, Eaton.'

Father's reply came by return of post:

'My very dear son,

*Many thanks for your letter received this am. I should like
to congratulate you on it. I have been feeling for the last few
days that I said more in my letter than I really intended and
if I said anything to hurt you, I apologize . . . .*

*Anyhow, thank God, we are not parting "brass rags" as
I feel when once you reach the Emerald Isle we shall not see
much more of each other, as I think you know my utter
detestation of flying or perhaps funk is the right word to use!*

*Mum joins me in love to you all and my earnest wish is
that you make a better success of this farming game than I
did! Come and see us soon.'*

Meanwhile back in Cerne Abbas we had engaged Messrs
Pickford & Co to move us. They told us they worked in
conjunction with Coras Impair Eirreann, the Irish State
Transport company. Pickfords would pack our belongings at
Cerne Abbas and convey everything to Heysham where the
consignment would be put on board the ferry for Belfast. C.I.E.
would then collect the pantechnicon at Belfast and deliver our
furniture and belongings to us at Ballyknockan. They would
inform us by telephone when we might expect the delivery.
Before our departure from England we purchased a new carpet
which would fit exactly into the dining room of our new home.

Imagine our dismay when we finally arrived at Ballyknockan to find the Flannerys still in residence. Nothing had been moved so we spent the first two nights with Mr and Mrs Jack Laurie who kept a guest house not far away. Soon after the departure of the Flannerys we received a visit from a complete stranger who had called with his sow to be put to the Flannery's boar. We had agreed to 'mind' the boar till Mr Flannery was in a position to collect and house it on his new property near Redcross but we had not bargained for this request. After some thought on the matter I decided not to comply with this request but to enquire of Larry Flannery when I saw him on the morrow. The caller's name was Macdonald so that well-known nursery rhyme came into my mind about Old Macdonald had a Sow, with a snort, snort here and a snort, snort there! Also whilst settling in, another incident occurred for which I had not bargained. There was a field of hay bales which had been made by Liam Clarke who had taken the field on conacre from the Flannerys. Liam had sold this field of hay bales and the person who had bought it came to collect. The field was approached through gate pillars, known in the district as Parnell Pillars after the famous (infamous?) MP who lived near Rathdrum and who had blotted his copy book at the end of the last century through his association with Kitty O'Shea. One evening there was a knock at the door and there on the doorstep was a person whom I had not seen before — the person who had come to collect the hay bales. He informed me that whilst coming through the gateway with a load of hay bales on his trailer, he had inadvertently knocked down one of my pillars. I went out to the scene of the accident and there were the remains of the pillar, consisting of huge stone blocks, lying on the ground. He promised to build the pillar again as good as new. When I came to survey the damage more thoroughly I realized that the total width of the trailer and its load was far more than the width of the gateway — in fact the load was nearly two feet wider than the width of the gateway! The unloaded trailer would *just go through* the gateway and this was presumably the logic of the operation! Anyway he was as good as his word and in two days time our pillar was restored as good as new if not better.

I was in need of assistance on the farm and Francis Lee was recommended to me by Liam Clarke. Francis Lee (or Frank as he was known locally) lived about a mile away with his brother. They had a small holding on which they ran about five or six milch cows and Frank and his brother went out to work after seeing to their stock. I interviewed Frank for the job of general farm worker and he seemed to be just the right type of man for which we were looking. He had a driving licence, was conversant with most types of farm machinery (which I most certainly was not, though I did not tell him!), was intelligent and obviously strong. I offered him the rate of pay pertaining to general agriculture workers of the day, namely ten pound per week which he accepted with the proviso that, if I wanted him to operate machinery then the rate for the job was an extra ten shillings! I agreed but there was a snag. Frank did not believe in paying Income Tax and was quite adamant on this point. If I wanted him then his pay was to be net of tax. He was quite prepared to pay for an Insurance Stamp but Income Tax — NO. That was not for the likes of him. That was for people who could afford it! There was obviously nothing for it but to agree to pay the tax element for him. That in fact put his wages up to ten pounds thirteen shillings per week. Frank was happy but I, as the boss, had to lump it but he turned out to be a reliable employee and, provided one jollied him along, he was cheerful and efficient. Anyway I had a worker on the farm who seemed to know what he was talking about.

I had discussed the future with Mary and we both agreed that we would give the place a maximum of seven years and that if we could not see a substantial profit by the time those years were up, then we would sell up and think again. Seven years were sufficiently far ahead not to bother us as to what those 'new pastures' might be. There was a job to be done here and now. After all, I had made a success of the jobs I had tackled so far so let's look on the bright side and get stuck in. What was it that father had said — 'Farming is one of the easiest ways to lose your capital.' Right Dad, we'll show you! We'll make a success of this enterprise as we have done with the previous ones and I reckon I have done my sums right.

One of the first things to do was to get some stock on the land so, together with Frank, I went off to Aughrim Mart to buy. We entered that winter with twenty store bullocks which I proposed to out-winter in the 'lawn' field close to the house. If the winter weather turned too hard we could house them in the old milking parlour though it would be a tight squeeze. We saw the two boys off to school from Dublin airport later that month — the fare from Dublin to Exeter, a through flight in those days by 'Herald' aircraft was thirty pounds each return!

That first winter, January 1968, it started to snow. Frank came down on the Sunday morning to see if we were all right and fortunately we had plenty of fodder in stock so we fed the cattle along the line of the hedge in the lawn field. There was plenty of work for us all — hedging and ditching, fencing and clearing the out-houses of manure, and repairing roofs in the yard. In the bungalow there was plenty of work too. Walls required painting and the whole bungalow had to be carpeted. Here we were lucky in having a friend in Dorothy Saul who had been a school friend of Mary's. Dorothy's husband had passed away many years before leaving her to run the family hardware business in Rathdrum. Her son, Brian, was not interested in the business so Dorothy had put it on the market. Meanwhile she had given us an introduction to a firm of wholesale carpet suppliers so we were able to get the whole bungalow professionally carpeted at wholesale prices. Mary ran up the curtains — a job at which she was particularly adept as she was a very good needle woman and was quite used to making all our curtains.

I made full use of the Agricultural Instructors and received much useful advice from them which I followed, particularly as regards the grasslands which had been overgrazed and were badly in need of fertilizers. I decided to put some twenty acres down to hay and I also sowed about twenty acres of barley which job I entrusted to my neighbour, Jimmy Condell. I was gradually building up a range of implements and had purchased a Ford 3000 Tractor as well as a Ransome three-furrow Plough and a Welger Trailer which could be adapted with the aid of side screens into a silage trailer as well as a manure spreader. Frank showed me how to plough a straight furrow and all-in-all life was being kind to us. The cattle were thriving and the Ballyknockan grass which was obviously of good quality was responding to our care and attention. Our crops grew and ripened and Liam Clarke was engaged to come in to Combine and sell our barley crop which yielded well.

At the end of the summer term 1968 Patrick left All Hallows School and obtained a scholarship to Gurteen Agricultural College in County Offaly where he was to spend two years.

During his time there, the college opened a new accommodation block for students and this was duly opened by the then Minister for Agriculture, Neil Blaney. Mr Blaney was later to leave the Fianna Fail party and was to sit as an independent member for Donegal. Personally I did not care much for Mr Blaney as I felt he was up to his neck in sympathy for the IRA and was in cahoots with Charles Haughey.

My father was most impressed when told of Patrick's scholarship. 'He is the first Davy ever to gain such a distinction.'

All seemed to be going well so we purchased forty young weanling lambs to eat off the stubbles from the barley fields and hopefully show us a profit after some weeks on our land. We did indeed sell them off in early February as fat lambs. All was going well when — horrors — Foot and Mouth Disease broke out in England in the autumn of 1968. The Irish authorities immediately put stringent restrictions into practice. No cattle were to be moved between farms and any cattle that were offered for sale through a Mart *had to be sold* and could not be brought back to the farm. Any visitors to the farm had to pass through a disinfectant bath and this applied both to foot as well as vehicular traffic. In fact visitors were not to be encouraged at all and each and every farmstead became a virtual island within its own boundary fence!

There is a proverb which states: 'What is sauce for the goose is sauce for the gander'. That proverb certainly held good so far as we were concerned for, as soon as Foot and Mouth Disease had been confirmed in England, cattle prices began to rise in Ireland and beef cattle were in great demand. Prices for good quality stock virtually doubled overnight so that by the time the winter months were over the cash value of bullocks had almost doubled when I came to sell them out. It did not take much power of observation to realize that accommodation for livestock was woefully lacking and also that it would be impossible to winter any great number of cattle outside as I had done with my initial purchase of twenty head. I therefore ordered a sixty by thirty feet hay barn together with a sixty by thirty feet lean-to to be erected adjacent to the old milking parlour so that I was able to make use of an old lean-to shed that was already in position next door. I set Frank on to digging holes to take the twelve uprights but after a day or two I soon realized that the job would take him at least three weeks to complete. I could not afford this lapse of time and Frank was not very pleased at being given 'hard labour'. I therefore engaged the services of the local contractor, Robert Condell, who had the holes dug in three days! The erectors arrived soon after the shed was delivered and the whole new complex was up and ready for the builders within a week. Meanwhile I had engaged a local builder to construct my new cattle yard consisting of a silage pit in the hay barn and a lying-in shed for the cattle in the adjacent lean-to. Outside the built-in area there was to be an exercise yard and collecting pen, and the entire structure of silage pit, lying-in shed, concrete bases to all areas, exercise yard and collecting pen, all of which covered an area of approximately ten thousand square yards cost me a fraction over £2,000! This was, in fact, largely met out of the profits on my first wintering of twenty head of bullocks and was largely due to the outbreak of Foot and Mouth Disease which had pushed up the prices of livestock in Ireland.

I learned something about the Irish tradesman's character during this operation and that was: never take a statement he may make too literally. During the course of the building work on my new cattle yard, the builder and his men had a disconcerting habit of disappearing for two or three days without any warning. This became somewhat irksome so I asked him to let me know beforehand when he was likely to be away. This was when I rumbled him. He was, of course, engaged on another job and was trying to keep both of his customers happy. After my protests, he would come to me and say, for example: 'We shall not be here until Thursday.' Thursday would come and there would be no sight nor sound of the builders. I quickly learned to ask which Thursday he was talking about and from then onwards everything went well!

In anticipation of having a full shed of cattle the following winter I ordered a single chop Taarup Forage Harvester for delivery in time for silage making. This machine duly arrived in late May and we were all set for putting the enterprise into operation. I calculated that the pit, measuring as it did some sixty feet by thirty feet by nine feet high would hold about 360 tons of silage if we could get it full and this, I estimated, would feed thirty head of young cattle for about five months. This feed would have to be supplemented by hay and, if necessary, some fattening nuts. These nuts would only be fed to those cattle that were first for the market, the remainder would be turned out to grass and would be finished on the first flush of spring grass which came fairly early at Ballyknockan. Our first winter's operations were successful but we had trouble with the disposal of slurry. That winter was particularly wet and windy and there was a great deal of slurry to dispose of. A Yard Scraper had to be purchased and we were able to keep the yard reasonably clean by pushing all the slurry into one corner. The next problem was frozen pipes. The water pipes frequently froze until I hit on the idea of piling the manure and slurry up against the water pipes which fed the troughs from outside the yard.

Silage making is hard work particularly when it came to spreading the grass in the pit. We had friends in Rathdrum named Whelan. Tim was an ex-Indian Police Officer and he thoroughly enjoyed helping me on the farm. He was not a young man but he seemed to have an inexhaustible supply of energy and would work away for hours with a pike, spreading each load as it was delivered and tipped. When all was safely gathered in, rolled down tight and covered with a sheet of plastic, we had to give some thought to a barrier or some such means of restraining the cattle from eating their heads off. We decided to purchase three ten-foot Silage Barriers for this purpose and once electric light was installed we were ready for wintering our cattle. The whole installation and structure was successful but I was not happy with the silage barriers. They were heavy and cumbersome to move and they had to be moved every day as the cattle ate their way through the silage. Something had to be done about that before the following winter — we were all right regarding the hay racks because they were strategically sited on the party wall between the silage pit and the lying-in yard so all we had to do was drop the hay into the racks from above. We stored bales of straw two deep on top of the silage and the weight of these helped to compress the silage as well as preventing the wind from blowing under the polythene sheeting. We were thus able to drop the bedding into the shed and the hay into the racks from above which reduced the labour involved and proved very handy at weekends when Frank was off! I was able to connect into the electricity supply to the yard so we soon had the wintering shed illuminated after dark. As there was a certain amount of vandalism going on in the district we used to leave the light burning all night to deter any 'baddies' who happened to have targeted our yard! We came through our sojourn at Ballyknockan without any unwelcome visitors who may have had malicious intent.

My sister Eve who was ill with cancer, was being looked after by our half-aunt Muriel Bibby at the latter's home and we heard in February that Eve was far from well and was virtually confined to bed. Mary and I flew over to Manchester and thence on by train to Sheffield to visit her. We found her in fairly good spirits though obviously the cancer had got a firm hold. Her eyes were sunken and her complexion was yellow but she was still able to joke about the fact that she now had the Travers liver! This was an allusion to mother who, when feeling under the weather, would say she was suffering from Travers liver! Eve also pointed out that Mother no longer had a monopoly on liver trouble!

We went by train to Bournemouth to spend a few days with my parents before returning to Ballyknockan. In answer to our suggestion that they should go up to Sheffield to see Eve, they said they were quite unable to face up to a visit to see her although Eve had put all her remaining strength and effort into having them to stay for the previous Christmas, and doing all the Christmas cooking.

On our return home I immediately set to work to prepare for our new cattle yard and it was whilst working on the site during the latter part of March that we heard that Eve had passed away. Mary and I flew over for the funeral which was very well attended, for the Sandford family was an old and much respected Sheffield family.

19

During the year 1969 we had various visitors to stay with us including my brother-in-law Geoffrey Sandford together with his two sons (my nephews) Andrew and Stephen, aged at that time fourteen years and twelve years. In April of that year there was a Horse and Pony Sale in the Livestock Mart at Ashford and, for the sum of ninety Guineas, I purchased a four year-old fourteen hand gelding, named Billy. I suppose this was an impulse purchase but I felt he might be useful for riding round and checking the livestock. I also hoped that one of the boys might take to riding and a pony of this size would be ideal for starters. Billy was quiet and easily caught and when Mary and I went to England for a short holiday, Pam Lindars who lived at Castle Howard, Avoca offered to have him for the use of the children of her farm manager, Billy Morrisey. On our return Pam Lindars offered to buy the pony as he was just the right mount for her manager's children and I agreed to let her keep him for the same money as I had paid for him. Meanwhile I was interested in and bought a seven year-old fifteen hand mare. My reasoning being that she was a nice, comfortable ride and she would also make a good brood mare in time to come. She did, in fact, throw me two nice foals — the first a filly and the second a colt. The mare cost me £200. I sold the filly foal for £100 and subsequently sold the mare with her colt foal at foot for £200. I reckon I was out of pocket but 'you can't win 'em all!'

We received several visits from Ted Scott and family as we were handily placed for dinner, bed and breakfast for anyone who wanted to visit Dublin. Their son, Guy, was at school at Aravon Preparatory School in Bray so we were useful in this respect.

By the time 1970 came in we were well and truly ensconced

in our new way of life and were enjoying every minute of it. We seemed to have been accepted in the neighbourhood and soon learned the way of things as far as the locals were concerned. It was in this year that I purchased an out farm at Ballyteigue. This holding consisted of a small, single storey bungalow (or Irish-type farm house) on forty-eight acres, of which about eight acres were bogland. I resolved to drain what I could of the bogland and put the rest down to forestry, or perhaps offer it to the forestry if the price were right. I did, in fact, offer the bog to the forestry department but they would pay only ten pound per acre which I did not feel was good enough. The whole property was in a run down state having previously belonged to the Condells and the house was in need of paint as well as modernization and I started by re-wiring the interior and I put in a ring circuit myself which was interesting and fun! After all the titivations were finished we let the house as a holiday home and met a number of interesting people as a result. We charged forty pounds per week and the house could sleep six persons with no problem. The only snag was the water supply which was from a deep well in the front of the house which did, in fact, dry up on one occasion when we had the misfortune to let the house to a family from Birmingham. They arrived at one am and consisted of ten persons — having booked for a party of six people! Two of the party were young ladies in their teens who persisted in washing their hair at every opportunity. They, together with numerous baths enjoyed by other members of the party, caused the well to run dry and we had endless trouble in keeping them supplied with water. We had to utilize our water trailer to keep them supplied with water. We bought and delivered a supply of bread, butter and milk to start them off and were never paid for these goods, and they left at the conclusion of their stay without paying for the electricity they had used. We were out of pocket on that occasion and carefully vetted any future applicants and had no more trouble.

In 1970 an attractive farm property known as Ballard and situated in the hills behind our village of Ballinaclash, came on the market. It belonged to a man named Kinsella in Carlow and was on the market for £15,000. It consisted of a two storey house, partly renovated, on seventy-five acres of quite good land although the average height above sea level was about 700 feet.

None of the fields were watered (which was a good bargaining point!) but it would seem to have potential if one could get it at the right price, say £12,000. Anyway it would seem to be a good investment. After due deliberation and consultation with my brother-in-law, Ted Scott, I put in a bid on behalf of the boys' Trust, at £12,000 and eventually got it for £12,500. A great deal of work was wanted both on the house and on the farm but I felt it would be a useful adjunct to our farm at Ballyknockan and would also give the boys a stake in the country and also in the district. To finance this purchase I regret I had to disobey one of my father's strictures in the Trust Deed in which he stated that no funds were to be invested in the Irish Republic. Was this an investment — well, it depends what you mean by investment, doesn't it? Up to that point I had followed these instructions to the letter but in this case I felt the opportunity was too good to miss. As things turned out I was right in my surmise. As the local trustee it was incumbent on me to gain the maximum return from this investment and we managed to let the house for four pounds per week with the tenant paying the outgoings. The land and buildings we kept for ourselves.

I put a great deal of my own money into the farm. The water supply, for instance was from a deep well and fed direct to the house and yard only — there was no supply to any of the fields. I installed a pressure tank for the pump as well as a new water tank in the roof of the house as I soon discovered that the existing tank was rusted through. I installed water troughs in the covered yard and laid plastic pipes to all the fields to serve drinking troughs which I also purchased. I also bought and erected gates to all the fields. All in all I must have spent close on a thousand pounds on the place out of my own pocket and luckily it was stock proof and ready to farm. After the installation of a cattle crush made from concrete blocks and the erection of a skulling gate, the yard was ready for wintering stock. Ballard proved a very useful outfarm for us as well as giving the sons a place of their own on which to graze cattle and sheep. The land was fertile and produced some excellent crops of corn and hay for us. It was whilst gathering and stacking the hay crop in 1972 that I heard from my mother that my father was very ill and would I come over immediately. Mary had taken the message so I left the job at once to Patrick and a lad whom we had

159

engaged from Gurteen Agricultural College and made preparations to fly over to England the next day. I found Father to be bed-ridden and he was now attended by two private nurses by day and one by night. I would add here that way back in the April of 1972 I had arranged for his Medical Insurance with BUPA to be paid in full so that there were no further calls for Premiums and also that Father had made me his Proxy to attend to all his financial affairs so that each and every month when I made my visits I would clear all outstanding accounts and thus leave Mother with no worries on that score — she had an account in her own right which was fed automatically from Father's account at the bank. There was little I could do apart from keeping Mother company, taking her out for runs in the car and to occasional meals which made a change for her as she was no longer able to drive the car. When the week was up I decided to return home: I had a farm to run and it was getting on for harvest time. Came the morning for my departure and Mother threw one of her fainting fits in the kitchen. She had begged me to stay a little longer but I felt that if I acquiesced to this suggestion it would be all the more difficult to get away. I therefore stuck to my guns and this was when Mother threw her fainting fit but not before she had called me a heartless boy and so on. This remark I found rather hurtful but I understood her distress and tried to explain that I was on the end of the telephone and could be with her within a few hours. I still carry in my memory the sight of Mother on the doorstep as my taxi drew away, with an expression of utter hopelessness and despair on her face. But what else could I do? We all have our lives to lead and we must face up to whatever fate has in store for us. We know not what the morrow may bring — and just as well too! Mary met me at Rathdrum station after I called her from Dublin, and so we resumed our daily round.

Surprisingly, Mother was the first to pass away. On Saturday morning, 8 August the telephone rang and it was the Bournemouth doctor, Doctor Tolhurst, on the line. I was expecting a call but the news he broke to me had me absolutely shattered. He told me that my mother had passed away in the night: it was not Father after all though he was desperately ill and was not expected to last very much longer — two or three days perhaps. He had not been told of Mother's passing and would I please come over right away. It appears that the night nurse had been expecting Mother's usual visit to Father at about seven o'clock to share a cup of tea with him. When she had not appeared by about seven fifteen am she had gone to Mother's bedroom and had found her sitting up in bed with her light on, a book in her hand, and lying back on the pillows dead. A subsequent post mortem revealed that she had suffered a massive coronary which must have occurred at about four thirty that morning. Tim Whelan came with us to the airport to bring the car back and I was so distressed that I failed to hear our flight being called. This just about finished me and if it were not for Mary who took control of the situation I do not know what would have happened. As it was she got us on Stand By and we were away on the next flight to London.

On arrival at the flat we found that Mother had been removed to the mortuary and my cousin, Cecile Van der Kiste, was holding the fort pending our arrival. Luckily the bedrooms in the flat were shut off from the main living quarters so the comings and goings were not heard by Father who would have been wondering what on earth was happening. We decided to leave him till morning when I had arranged for the doctor and also the vicar to call at ten o'clock at which time I would tell Father about Mother.

On the Sunday morning I went in to Father who was looking very frail indeed, and greeted him in the usual way. His first words after returning my greeting were:

'Have you seen your mother?'

I replied that I had not seen her and that was the reason I had come to see him. As he did not reply I referred to a conversation we had had together one evening when he and Mother were staying with us at Ballyknockan last summer. During that conversation he had asked me that, if anything were to happen to him, would we take care of Mother. He then went on to say that it was his hope that when their time was up, she would be taken first as she would be quite unable to cope on her own. Of course I assured him that we were always available to 'come to the rescue', that either of them could be sure of a roof over their head with us, and anyway this was a depressing conversation. Father had replied that it may be depressing but he wanted to be sure that Mother would be cared for in the case of such an eventuality. I used this chat as a lead in for the news I was about to impart to him.

'You remember the chat we had last year when you expressed the hope that Mother would be taken first?' I said to him. 'Well, your wish has been granted.'

'Is she dead?' he asked, his voice faint but firm.

'Yes,' I answered.

'Thank God,' he said with a sigh, and sank back on the pillows.

Almost at that moment there came a knock at the door and Dr Tolhurst appeared. I withdrew and listened at the door.

'Hello Doc,' whispered Father. 'I hope you're not going to keep me hanging around any longer?'

That all occurred on the Sunday morning.

My Father died at seven pm on Tuesday, 11 August and their joint funerals took place at St Peter's church on Thursday morning followed by cremation at the Bournemouth Crematorium in accordance with their wishes. Hugh Travers, who had travelled all the way down from East Bergholt in Suffolk spent the night with us and the Midland Bank Executors who were the executors for both their Wills were on the doorstep the next morning, almost before we had had time to realize what had happened! John Wansey who had married my second cousin Muriel Pettinger just before the war and to whose wedding I had gone, took the service with the vicar. The vicar, whose name I regret I have forgotten, was kindness itself and asked Mary and me round for tea, and I was able to give him a small cheque for 'church funds'. I was told later that he had been made a bishop. I hope this is right.

I must have been in a very 'over wrought' state for I can remember very little of what the Executors told us except for one thing that stands out in my memory. They explained the procedure involved in obtaining Probate for the Wills and then went on to say: 'You must remember that the Revenue Commissioners will expect persons such as your late parents will have a considerable amount of valuables such as jewellery.' After they had departed Mary and I set about sorting clothes and other items in the flat and I can remember collecting various items of jewellery together to take down to the executors. It was not until a few days later that I realized what I was doing and that I had parted with some items that I particularly wanted to keep. I got in touch with the executors and found that I had to *buy back* any pieces of jewellery that I wanted to keep and

162

that I had sent down to them in error. The two items which particularly concerned me were a brooch in the form of a Bee and a pair of diamond earrings made for pierced ears. Mary did not have pierced ears but was prepared to have them pierced in order to be able to wear those earrings! The two items were subsequently valued and deducted from my share of the estate — in other words I had paid for them! When eventually their two Wills were handed over to me I discovered two statements which completely upset all my plans. The first was a bequest by my grandmother (mother's mother) who had left a Heavy Victorian Diamond Brooch to my mother with the expressed wish that it should become a family heirloom. I had never seen my mother wearing this brooch and did not even know of its existence. It was a very heavy brooch made of large stones — a typical Victorian piece in fact — and both Mary and I had debated whether we should keep it and have it broken up into smaller objects but we decided against it. When I approached the executors I was told I was too late and that the 'return' had already been sent in. The next thing was a codicil executed by my father soon after the death of my sister Eve. I knew nothing of this codicil but it stated that in exercise of the powers conferred upon them they now wished that the Trust capital should be disposed as follows: The half share due to my sister Eve should be held on trust for her children until they became twenty-five years of age then they would be entitled to their share of the Marriage Settlement. The other half share to be held on trust and the income thereof paid to me for my lifetime and on my death, each of my children still living at the time of my death to share the capital. This Indenture, or re-arrangement of affairs was understandable but it threw into complete disarray all my planning over the recent years for I had planned my life on the assumption that come the death of the survivor of my parents I would come into a half share of the capital of the Marriage Settlement. By that time I had assumed that I would be in a position to hand over the farm at Ballyknockan to my two sons and build a bungalow for Mary and me on the land, (I had in fact already earmarked the plot!), and that we would be there if and when we were wanted, either for advice or relief purposes. Alas for the best laid plans! This development put an entirely different complexion on the future and I would have to do some rethinking as to where I should go from here. My first action was to go and see David Preston, the family's solicitor who had been responsible for drawing up the Indenture in the first place. I put it to him that I should have been told about this alteration but he replied to the effect that he did not consider it to be his duty to interfere in a family matter. I told him that I considered it a matter of business in these enlightened times and that it was his duty as a lawyer to explain the possible consequences of the actions of my parents. He disagreed so the matter was left. My position was now rather difficult as I had been putting all my resources back into the farm, in the belief that I would eventually inherit my share of the settlement capital. That capital to which I had been looking for relief was no longer to be made available. I had put a lot of money into Ballyknockan as well as financing the capital requirements of my sons' farm at Ballard and here I was 'wi' nowt' as they say in Yorkshire. My father had left me a legacy of one thousand pounds and this I utilized to finance an extension to the bungalow so that we now had a self-contained guest wing with bathroom and lavatory en suite. It is a reflection on the way things have gone that in the year 1972 I was able to put on a wing to the bungalow and to carpet and curtain it all within the one thousand pounds!

We had a large amount of livestock on the farm by this time and we had switched from fattening bullocks to running a suckler herd. We had over one hundred head of cattle of one sort or another on the farm at Ballyknockan as well as eighteen followers on the boys' land at Ballard. One of our suckler cows had calved and had too much milk for her one calf so we bought a pedigree bull calf to put on to her. This calf had tight ligaments in his fore feet which meant that his feet were permanently bent backwards. Patrick worked hard at these and eventually they came right and we had him registered as a bull by the Department of Agriculture. Once this was done we turned him out with the eighteen heifers which were grazing on the Ballard land and he put them all in calf for us.

By this time Richard had gained sufficient 'A' levels for entry to the Royal Agricultural College, Cirencester and he was there studying the course for the Higher National Diploma which he obtained in 1974. Patrick at this time had a job with a dairy farmer at Mountrath and there met up with the Irish girl whom we had employed several years before as a mother's help. This girl was now married and settled in Mountrath with a swarm of children — as a good catholic should!

In mid-1972 we acquired a West Highland White Terrier puppy which we christened 'Penny' because it was about the time that Britain and Ireland adopted decimal currency. This entailed the scrapping of most of the old coins and the introduction of new ones as replacements, amongst which was the New Penny.

20

Ireland was now in the European Common Market and prices had started their now familiar upward spiral. Animal feed and land fertilizers all shot up in price and land prices, too, had taken off. As far as we were concerned the warning lights were starting to flash and the year 1973 would be a crucial one for us as far as finances were concerned. I had already realized that our farm would not carry the whole family and the farm at Ballard was not large enough to provide a decent living for my two sons. We had been thwarted in our effort to expand at Ballyknockan when we were unable to succeed in buying a neighbouring farm just up the road from us. This farm of about sixty acres was owned by a Mr Kenny whom I had got to know. The dwelling was a bungalow with a corrugated iron roof and had come on to the market in 1970 for sale by Public Auction. It would have made a perfect adjunct to our main holding at Ballyknockan if we could get it at a reasonable price. I had walked the land and had found there was a lot of marginal land as well as several acres of scrub/gorse which would have to be cleared in order to be brought into production. I put a mental price of £50,000 on it and Mary and I went to the auction at the Grand Hotel in Wicklow conducted by Clarke, Delahunt & Co., the local auctioneers and estate agents. The bidding started at £30,000. We dropped out at £50,000 and it was finally sold to the Crammonds for something like £65,000. At this time there was a fairly strong feeling abroad, particularly among the Celtic league composed of ardent Nationalists, against the holding of excessive amounts of land and I was very gratified one day when I went to the livestock mart at Aughrim to be greeted by two Irishmen at the entrance gate who commiserated with me over our failure to get the Kenny land.

'You should have had that land,' they said.

On reflection, I believe we were considered as suitable residents in the area because Mary was Irish and we were all of us prepared to take our coats off and work our land. Towards the end of 1973, in November actually, we decided that the future in farming in Ireland was too uncertain and that we had best cash-in whilst the going was good. We asked Harry Delahunt, the senior partner in the local firm of Estate Agents, to look over our property and he put a value at auction of £100,000 on it! We gave him the job! After the usual advertising, the auction was held and the highest bid was £65,000 which we naturally refused. After the abortive auction, a Mr Appleton from England offered us £90,000 subject to Land Commission approval. We accepted this offer without much hope of success as the Land Commission were not very keen on the English acquiring land in Ireland, and as expected the said Land Commission finally turned the Appletons down. I seem to remember we had to wait for some three or four months before their decision came through. Anyway we were able to pocket the interest on the Appleton's deposit. It was now February 1974 and we were due to complete the purchase of Ballyteigue House on 31 March. As luck would have it, a Mr Cribben who was a dentist from the Dublin area, came on the scene. He had recently sold some highly valuable land on the outskirts of Dublin and was anxious to place his money in land and was introduced to us through Clarke, Delahunt & Co. He became rather a nuisance as he would invariably call after having a drinking session down at Phelan's Bar in the village where he was busily sounding out all about us and our land. Apparently the locals spoke well of us for he finally made a bid of £80,000 for our property. This was not really good enough as land prices had by now taken off and good land was fetching anything up to £750 per acre. I went to see Harry Delahunt and in my presence he rang Mr Cribben and we concluded a sale at £88,000. Twelve thousand short of the one hundred thousand suggested by Harry but a good profit all the same and I was now able to conclude the purchase of Ballyteigue House. We had made it by the skin of our teeth and moved in to Ballyteigue House on 1 April. Before leaving Ballyknockan we had a sale of all our livestock and surplus machinery and I gave certain equipment to my sons for use on their farm at Ballard. Included in this 'gift' were a

Ford 4000 Tractor and a Silage/General Purpose trailer. The Ballyteigue property consisted of a two-storey residence on approximately ten acres of land of which about one acre was formal garden. There was a yard some distance from the house which was tarmacadammed and consisted of a garage, an open barn, and four loose boxes. The yard entrance was either through large double gates from the roadway or else from the adjacent field. We moved all our farm machinery up to Ballyteigue House and were fortunate in this respect in that our new home was only about one mile away. We took over the staff from the Hartshorns, namely Kathleen in the house and Pat Hanrahan in the garden. The latter had had a hip operation on his left hip some years before but although he walked with a slight limp this did not appear to restrict him in his activities in the garden. Rather than lead a life of idle leisure I decided to set myself up as an Agricultural Contractor as I had retained most of my machinery so I advertised my services in the local weekly newspaper, *The Wicklow People*. I was kept busy all the first summer, mowing and making hay and silage but come the autumn there was not much doing so I went into partnership with John Macgregor whom I knew from my attendance at the IFA meetings. I bought a Ford County Tractor, a Rotovator and a Deep Furrow Plough and we were called on for numerous reclamation works in the area. We called ourselves Arthur Davy & Sons — a bit of sentimentality — and I borrowed the money for these heavy pieces of machinery from the Bank of Ireland Finance Company. At the end of a year I realized that there was not much to be gained from this enterprise so I gave it up. I was the employer and paid John two pound per hour as operator and driver and after meeting the monthly payments on the bank loan and paying my partner for his work, there was little if anything left in the kitty for me so I soon bailed out. Also, the Tractor was a Condell cast-off; it drank oil and was in a pretty ropey condition so I was lucky to dispose of the whole unit to a Contractor from Shilleleagh at the same price I had given for it. I repaid the bank what I still owed them and breathed a sigh of relief, resolving not to get involved with Condell cast-offs again. I was also finding it difficult to get paid for my services by a few farmers so, after two years, decided that the hassle was not worth while and gave it all up.

In January 1977 Mary discovered a lump in her left breast

and a cancer was diagnosed. She went into hospital for the operation and a full scale mastectomy was performed on her. This was a traumatic experience for her and me but she made a rapid recovery and was home again after about two weeks. She had to go to St Luke's hospital to see Dr O'Halloran every month for some six months and this entailed having chemotherapy treatment which made her feel pretty awful. Matters were not made any easier for us by a strike of petrol delivery drivers so it became difficult to obtain supplies. She made very good progress throughout that summer so that, come the autumn, I was able to suggest to her that we should go to Australia to visit her sister and to help her sister, Betty, and her husband, Len, celebrate their twenty-five years out there. I knew she was anxious to do this and as I had hoped, she jumped at the idea. Dr O'Halloran gave us his approval so I made arrangements to travel out there in the following spring with a stopover in Singapore for four nights. We left home on 6 February en route for London Heathrow and spent the night at the Eccleston Hotel in Eccleston Square, not far away from the coach terminal. We had decided to travel over to London the day before as there were so many imponderables to consider — lightening strikes, weather and so forth — and we did not want there to be any hitches.

After a comfortable night at the hotel we reported at the coach terminal where we booked in and were allotted seats in the non-smoking section of the aircraft which we learned was to be a Jumbo Jet (Boeing 747) of Singapore Airlines. Our route out was via Amsterdam, Paris, Rome, Cairo, Bombay and we finally arrived at Singapore at six o'clock the following evening. The cabin crew on Singapore Airlines were very good indeed and I discovered that Champagne (free) for breakfast was an excellent 'pick-me-up!' We were booked for the four nights at the Holiday Inn. We made the error in falling for a conducted tour of the city on the evening of our arrival so at about ten pm a Mr Erskine arrived to pick us up for a tour of the bright and not so bright lights! The tour was rather a farce really. We did see one or two unusual sights, including a Chinese funeral parlour complete with corpse and we also partook of a rice and prawn dish whilst watching a disgusting display of sexual depravity by some white men who were obviously perverts and enjoyed sexual satisfaction by appearing in the nude and performing various acts of buggery. There were only two other couples on the tour and we were none of us sufficiently alert to take in what was shown to us. We were returned to our hotel at about two am and slept the sleep of the just. I slept till lunch time and went down to the Coffee Shop for breakfast only to be told that breakfast was long past and that they were now serving lunch!

After breakfast the next day we went out to explore the city. The first thing we noticed was the humidity. The air hung like a blanket around us and we were unable to go far on foot without feeling tired and limp. However we *did* reach the bazaar where all sorts of temptations were on display. I was tempted by a Japanese camera at £170 which I knew for a fact was priced at over £250 at home in Dublin. Mary was captivated by some delightful Kaftans in a variety of beautiful colours and designs. I managed to persuade her to have a Kaftan made specially for her which would be ready the same evening. She succumbed and the resultant article was most becoming. She wore it a lot in Australia and it looked very smart on her. I bought myself a Seiko wrist watch which I still use to this day.

I had an ex-army friend who had settled in Borneo and I had written to him suggesting we meet in Singapore. However, when we arrived there was a letter from him to say that he had not been well but that he had given our name to the Head Porter of the hotel who had promised to look after us. I was very disappointed not to be meeting David Ross after all these years — Mary was disappointed too as he had stayed with us in Sheffield many years before when he was an influential official with the Sultan of Borneo and had been awarded the Order of the White Elephant!

The onward journey to Sydney, also by Singapore Airlines jumbo jet, went without incident and, after a short stop at Jakarta in Indonesia we flew direct and overnight to Sydney where we arrived at ten am. Customs formalities were soon completed and then came the problem of finding accommodation. There was a Tourist Accommodation desk in the airport foyer so thither we directed our footsteps and found a very helpful lady who soon fixed us up with a twin room at the Manhattan Hotel in the Kings Cross district of Sydney. We discovered later that Kings Cross district was somewhat similar to Soho in London and was also known to be frequented by ladies of easy virtue! We sent a telegram to Betty and Len and awaited developments which were not long in coming. A telegram was awaiting us on the second day which contained instructions to proceed to Newcastle by train where they would meet us. We booked our ticket and baggage for the following day. In Australia you book your luggage through to your destination, hand it over at the time of departure, and thus you travel light. Your baggage is unloaded and awaiting you at the other end. The train journey from Sydney to Newcastle lasts about four and a half hours and a trolley laden with beer and sandwiches patrols the length of the train and about ten minutes before arrival a loudspeaker system announces to all passengers the name of the forthcoming station and the approximate time of arrival.

We did not have long to wait before Betty and Len arrived to collect us and we were off and away. We spent one night en route at a Travel Lodge and very heavy rain fell that night. So heavy was the rain that when we neared Woolgoolga the road was under several inches of water. Len got out and pioneered the route for us while we had to lift our feet from the floor as the water came in through the door sill! Not to worry! It seems the Australian is used to this sort of thing and anyway the car soon dries out in the heat.

The Harrison's bungalow was built on stilts and was a mile or two outside Woolgoolga. Rain water was caught from the roof and anywhere else that it could be channelled and was stored in a 2,000 gallon tank beneath the patio from whence it was pumped, by an electric pump, as and when required. Just like it is in the country of Ireland! We spent two weeks with the Harrisons during which time we bathed in the sea (watch out for sharks) and roamed the countryside (watch out for snakes). Len advised us to make a noise as we walked through the bush to warn any snakes of our approach and they would thus have time to slip away!

From Emerald Beach, the district in which the Harrisons lived, we drove up to Brisbane to visit their children, Michael and Patricia and from Brisbane we flew up to Cairns to visit the Barrier Reef. We landed by boat on Green Island, one of only two genuine coral islands so we were told, and looked at coral and tropical fish through a glass-bottomed boat. We saw a giant clam reputed to be 150 years old. The colours of the fish and the coral were quite enchanting, quite unlike anything one has seen before in the Northern Hemisphere. From Cairns we took a Pioneer Coach trip up into the Tablelands passing through thick tropical rain forests which were a tangled mass of verdant forest and seemed to be quite impenetrable. The soil up on the Tablelands is volcanic and highly fertile and the climate is very moist. The chief crops grown are tea and tobacco to which the climate is most suitable. We returned to Cairns by way of the mountain railway which runs down through the Barron Gorge. This railway was built originally to supply the mines which were to be sunk up in the Tablelands and were to extract gold from a deposit which was found up there. However, when it came to the point it was found that there were insufficient deposits in situ to make the project worthwhile so the whole scheme was abandoned! A vast amount of money must have been expended on the railway which was about thirty kilometres in length and which now forms a popular tourist attraction. We had intended to go to Alice Springs and Ayers Rock but there had been very bad weather and much flooding so that part of our 'tour' had to be abandoned.

During the course of our trip to Queensland we came across an example of Aussie prejudice. We came down to breakfast one morning and joined two Malaysian girls at a table. They were nurses from Kuala Lumpur and were on holiday in Australia. They were waiting for service but as soon as Mary and I arrived and took the vacant seats at their table the waitress asked us for our order. Enquiries revealed that the two girls had not been served so we referred the waitress to them. This caused a terrible hiatus because the waitress said they were OK and what did we want. We declined to give our order until the two Malaysian girls had been served and so a position of stalemate developed — all very embarrassing! Somehow the impasse was resolved and Mary suggested that the two girls should accompany us in future and we would look after them. Betty and Len were not amused and left us in no doubt that that sort of behaviour was not to be tolerated. We found the girls' company quite congenial as they were well educated and told us that they had found this attitude towards them all over Australia.

On our return to Brisbane we stayed with Michael and his wife Lis for a few days and then on to his sister Tricia and her husband Les. The latter's two boys, Andrew and Darren, were mad on cricket and kept me bowling at them for what seemed liked hours on end! They presented me with a cricket ball on our arrival and Mary received a bottle of toilet water. I returned the ball on our departure but Mary had found the toilet water very refreshing and had used it all! There was some alarm and despondency in the latter's household because a family of aborigines had moved into the house opposite: the Aussie is nothing if not racially conscious and this was a further example of their prejudice. Whilst in Brisbane we were entertained to dinner at the Wagga Wagga Cricket Ground by Michael. This ground is one of the Test Match venues and the pavilion was full of all sorts of interesting memorabilia for me. Gosh, it was hot and humid! Whilst staying with Mike and Lis we were introduced to Mud Crabs — a great delicacy with the Australians. I thought they tasted of — mud! Mike and Lis took us out for picnics and we savoured a deal of the Aussie way of life. Picnics consisted of taking a few slices of steak and bread and stopping at the first fireplace we came to. The countryside has any number of these picnic places and nearly all seem to have a gas-fired barbecue on which to cook your meal. They work by putting a coin in the slot — a jolly good idea!

After a few days back at Emerald Beach we booked ourselves a trip to the Flinders Ranges and set off by air to Sydney. There was a frequent air service run by the internal airline named Ansett which provided a regular air service between areas of most population. We had booked our trip through a local Travel Agent in Goffs Harbour but when we came to check in at Adelaide we found that the coach had already left. Frantic telephone calls ensued, the coach was finally located and we were sent off by taxi to catch it. The Flinders trip was full of interest and, apart from one other person, the party was composed entirely of Aussies. The coach was supposedly air conditioned but had seen better days and the heat and humidity were almost overpowering. Flinders Ranges spread some 600 kilometres inland and during the whole of the trip we hardly met a soul although in the days of prospecting in the 1870s there had been a lot of prospecting for copper. It was difficult to visualize how those prospectors lived, for the heat was terrific and there was little or no water apart from brackish water holes. We took a trip in a small Cessna aircraft to view the whole area from above and then it became possible to understand how the hills had been formed by the constant upheaval of the rock strata — this strata having been folded and refolded numerous times by the movement of the earth's crust. Such mineral deposits as there are, namely copper, gold, uranium have become so broken and split that there are insufficient concentrations to make mining worth while. On our return to Adelaide we saw the Royal Yacht *Britannia* tied up in the harbour and also caught a glimpse of HRH The Duke of Edinburgh returning from some function or other. We did not see Her Majesty who was busy elsewhere. We did a day tour of the Barossa Valley wine growing district and then went by air-conditioned coach to Melbourne which took ten hours with two stops! The route took us through mile upon mile of prairie lands — corn stubble as far as the eye could see. It was their autumn and the harvest had not long been gathered. I imagine it must bear a strong similarity to the mid-west in the USA.

After two days in Melbourne we moved on to Canberra where we were due to meet up with the Harrisons again. They had spent several years in Canberra when Len had been employed in the Australian navy as a naval architect. More endless miles of scrub and stubble! We visited the Australian parliament building and also the War Memorial which is most impressive.

After four hectic days in Canberra we were driven home via Hill End — a typical ghost town which between the years 1850-1872 had been a thriving gold mining centre with a population of over 8,000 souls. There are now about 170 persons there! It was here that the largest gold nugget ever found was unearthed and it weighed 650 lbs! We stayed at the Royal Hotel, run by a Mr Waterford and he told us his story. Apparently his great grandfather was the ploughman for Lord Waterford in Ireland and was deported for punching his employer. We did not discover what his crime had been but his three great-grandchildren had achieved eminence in their various fields: one was a top barrister, one a well known surgeon and our host who owned at least three hotels. The original convict took the name of Waterford as he did not know his own name!

After a few more days spent at Emerald Beach we started for home and travelled down to Sydney by train from Goffs Harbour. The fare was A\$21.50 Economy class or about £3.00 sterling! The date was 3 May and we were due to fly out on 9 May so we planned a real spending spree! We stayed again at the Manhattan Hotel in Kings Cross on a Bed and Breakfast basis at A$23.50 each per day and found it ideal for our purposes. We did the Rocks area, the site of the original landings, and the settlement at Port Jackson and had an interesting session with Mr Bob Patten, the licencee of the Argyle Tavern, who was a fifth generation Aussie. His great-great-grandfather was a junior officer in Governor Macquarie's regiment of foot and his great-grandfather was officer in charge of the horse transport with the expedition under Burke and Willis to explore the continent from south to north. On 6 May all Air Traffic Controllers went on strike indefinitely so that *all* air traffic came to a complete standstill. We were becoming financially embarrassed by this time as we had been living it up over the past few days. The hotel was very understanding and allowed us to keep our very nice room without any extra charge and we eventually got away on 15 May. I had pulled off one of my better pieces of acting and explained on the telephone to the Air Line office, with a sob in my voice, that we had two children at home who were expecting their Mummy and Daddy back, and what were we to say to them. Anyway it worked and we were put near the top of the queue and got away on 15 May. The return journey entailed four changes — Melbourne, Singapore, Amsterdam and London!

On arrival in London we hired a car and drove down to Devon where I was to collect a porcelain clock which Aunt Dorothy Richardson had left to me in her Will. Having collected the clock we headed back to Heathrow and finally reached home on 19 May — some three and a half months since setting off for Australia. Modern travel is all very well when everything goes according to plan but one cannot help the feeling that when you close the front door, when will you see it again! The whole trouble with strikes is that it is invariably the public who suffers whereas it should be the employer against whom the strike is aimed when all is said and done!

All was well when we reached home though we did find two rather disgruntled sons who felt they were getting nowhere fast. Ballard was too small for the two of them and they did not feel like working for someone else. In the autumn of that year Mary and I went for a short holiday to the Isle of Man and we thought how like County Wicklow it was. On our return we suggested to the boys that they might have a look there which they did.

As a result they bought for £50,000 Ballanayre Farm near Peel at a Coroner's Auction and we now have two Manx daughters-in-law and four Manx grandchildren! They sold out the farm at a good profit — Patrick now drifts along happily (I think) and Richard has landed himself a job as farm manager for Walter Gilbey MHK and is also his general dogsbody. Why is it that people with money have to have a dogsbody? — they feel it is *infradig* to do small jobs for themselves, I presume.

The purchase of Ballanayre Farm was not without some drama. We had been in touch with estate agents on the island for Mary and I had been thinking of going over there ourselves. When details of a certain farm came through the post I flew over there to have a look at it. It was not what was wanted but I did hear about Ballanayre so I had a look at that and then sent for one of the boys to come over and see for himself. Patrick was available and he flew in the day before the auction. We had a quick look round that evening and again the following morning and resolved to attend the auction. There was no house with the farm of 150 acres but that matter could be faced at a later date! In fact the farm house had been sold off to a Mr and Mrs Darricotte and the coach house had been converted to a small dwelling house and sold off to a family named Husband. I had done a bit of sleuthing on my own and discovered that land prices were much the same as in Ireland but I was unable to find out much about the marketing of produce except that there was quite a flourishing trade with Northern Ireland and the United Kingdom.

Patrick and I attended the auction and were amazed to see so many people there. We had absolutely no idea who they were or whether they were actively interested or just spectators. In fact we were quite unaware of anything Manx, so we just hoped for the best, having decided at lunch time that we would not pay any more than £60,000 as the question of accommodation had yet to be resolved. The bidding opened at £25,000 and proceeded by five thousand bids to forty thousand quite briskly. Here there was a pause and I decided to play it by Irish rules! As soon as a bid of forty-two was made I jumped in with forty-five thousand pounds. There was another long pause until a further bid raised the offer whereupon I immediately raised it to fifty thousand and the property was knocked down to us.

Shortly after the auction I was approached by two separate

persons, one asking whether I would be prepared to sell to him The Glen which ran down to the sea which I refused to do, and the other was Mr Husband who was the owner of the converted Coach House who wanted to know what sort of farming we planned as he was thinking of spending a large capital sum on building an additional room onto the house. He did not want to do this if our farming activities were going to interfere with the tranquillity he now enjoyed. I could see a chance here of acquiring the house so I replied by letter stating that my sons were going to run the farm (which was quite true) and that they were confirmed cattle men. I also stated that I knew that they were planning a silage layout in the yard but more than that I did not know! As I had hoped, a reply came back that he was not prepared to chance the future on the information I had given and that he was preparing to put the house on the market. After a suitable pause I wrote to Mr Husband expressing my regrets and hoping that he would give me first refusal should he decide to go ahead with the sale of the house. We eventually bought the house for £21,000 and gave it to the boys by Deed of Gift so that they now had a Residential Farm. When they came to sell the property it realized £160,000 after about two years ownership — not a bad investment!

Meantime, Mary and I decided that the boys would be better on their own so we put our own house on the market by auction and it realized £55,000, and we went back to County Cork having found a nice semi-rural residence on the outskirts of the village of Leap, some twenty-seven miles from Mary's old home at Harbour View, and about nine miles from Skibbereen. This house, called South View, was situated above the estuary and the view was breathtaking. One looked down the estuary towards Glandore and behind us rose a rocky hill so that there was little likelihood of any building to take place near us. Next door was a waste plot of land which we thought we could perhaps buy at a later date.

21

We were soon enveloped in church affairs as the Rector of the parish, who was also the Dean of Rosscarberry, called upon us soon after our arrival. His name was 'Peter' Fleming and it was his half-brother, Jimmy, who had married us at Rathclaren church nearly thirty years before. We acquired a small day-boat and met up with the neighbours who all seemed friendly, pleasant, and of the Protestant persuasion! The latter was important though neither of us paid much attention as to what was the persuasion of our neighbours: life is too short to be bothered by such 'trivialities!' That was our viewpoint, anyway. We lived in a Christian' society and tried to lead a Christian life ourselves — the 'politics' of religion did not impinge upon our daily life and we left that side of things to the bigots!

We had to wait until 1 April before we could take possession of our new home so after spending two weeks in a bungalow near Rathdrum loaned to us by Dorothy Saul, we set off for a motoring holiday on the continent. There had been a very severe winter in the northern hemisphere and when we arrived at Le Havre on the ferry from Rosslare we were surprised to see the countryside in a state of utter desolation. Concrete electric pylons were lying around and broken off at their bases, cider apple trees were stripped of their branches and some even with broken trunks where the arctic winds had sheered them in half. Such was the mess that when we arrived at Bernay some three hours drive from Le Havre, we were unable to get in because the hotel was full of electrical workers who were based in that area to do repairs and were likely to be there for some months ahead. We did find a bed for the night but not at the Grand Hotel which we had hoped for. We thence made our way down south via Poitiers and Limoges and it was here that we became lost. It was a Sunday so we stopped outside a supermarket in the middle of the town to ask the way to Tulle.

We struck lucky and were guided out of town by a lady with two children who set us off on the right road. We spent a few days in Carcassonne before moving on through Port Bou and thus into Spain where we planned to pass the Easter holiday at our apartment near Almunecar. We arrived there on Good Friday and found 'The World and His Wife' in residence. This was the first time we had spent a public holiday in Spain. Every single apartment was occupied by families, mostly Spanish, and their children made as much noise, if not more noise than a school playground at break time. And, of course, their daily routine is so different to ours — they rise late in the mornings and retire late at night and the children seem to follow a similar routine. I did take a tape recording of the cacophony of sound but, alas, I have accidentally washed it out. The return journey was by way of Madrid and Burgos, Biarritz and Versailles where we stayed for a few days to 'do' Paris: the Louvre, Eiffel Tower, Fontainebleau and so on.

We moved to our new home on 5 April and everything seemed set fair. We bought our boat and arranged for a mooring, made friends with the neighbours and were sufficiently close to Mary's old home without being in their pockets. We visited the boys in the Isle of Man and in the May of the following year we went on a church pilgrimage 'In the Footsteps of Saint Paul' to Greece and Rome. It was after this holiday that Mary's cancer started to reappear and in September when she went to see her specialist in Dublin, he confirmed that the disease had re-appeared and had spread to her pelvis. This was, of course, the cause of her periodic back pain and I was told by Dr O'Halloran that we had about two years left together. I have often wondered since that time whether I may not have been the unwitting cause of the re-activation and spread of the cancer for, quite early on in our sojourn down south, we had gone back to County Wicklow to collect the cat which we had left with Kathleen. After lunch at Cahir I had seen an antique shop and called Mary over to see something in the window — a rocking chair I believe it was. Whilst walking down the pavement she failed to notice a small step in the surface and fell on to her left knee cap. She was in terrible pain and we rushed on to Wicklow town to see our own doctor who pronounced a probably broken knee cap and advised an X-ray. Her knee cap was indeed shattered and she was kept in hospital at Dun Laoghaire for a week and was finally discharged with her leg in plaster. The Greek trip was in the nature of a convalescence. We made one more visit to our apartment in Spain and then came the business of disposing of it.

We had told the agents that we wished to sell and they had expressed an interest in it. They were German and wanted to pay us in Deutchmarks which suited us quite nicely as there were bound to be difficulties over currency. They gave us Dm 3,000 in cash as a deposit and said they would settle finally in the summer. They failed to come up with the money but they did find a Spaniard who worked in Granada and who wanted a holiday retreat on the coast. He was working for the Spanish Tourist Board in Granada and did not flinch when I told him the price, inclusive of furniture, fixtures and fittings, was 1,250,000 pesetas (one million two hundred and fifty thousand pesetas). I had left Mary in the care of her brother and sister-in-law at The Glen in the June of 1980 and flew off to Malaga to finalize the deal. Mrs Putzfeld, the wife of the German agent, drove me up to Granada and I presented the buyer's cheque at the bank for cash. The cheque was duly honoured and I left with the money in bank notes stuffed into a holdall and felt as though I were a bank robber! By the time the teller had returned from having the cheque certified, there was a queue of people formed up behind me and they all smiled and nodded at me as though it was an everyday occurrence! Perhaps it was!

Back we drove to Almunecar and it was now Friday. The banks shut at four pm and I was due to fly back home the next day. What to do with all this money? I settled our debts with the agents, kept a small sum for out-of-pocket expenses and rushed off to the bank with the balance of well over a million pesetas. I had never been a millionaire before and was not likely to be one again but the trouble was that the money, in pesetas and sitting in a bank in Spain, was not much use to us in Ireland. Here we were lucky again for I was acquainted with a retired commandant of the Irish army who had set himself up as an estate agent for Spain and was always in need of Spanish money. I unloaded our nest-egg through him and invested the proceeds in Irish government stocks which in turn showed us a small profit!

Mary's general health was, by now, rapidly deteriorating though she had been able to move about with the aid of a walking frame. I was forced to consider a wheel chair for her and we eventually acquired such a chair that winter. The two sons visited us with their wives over the New Year 1981 and I made use of them to help me bring our beds down to the dining room which we turned into a bedroom. Soon after Patrick's departure on 5 January I was awoken in the early hours by a terrifying crash — Mary had fallen out of bed and was lying on the floor, moaning. Somehow I lifted her back into bed where she lay in considerable pain and I called the doctor. Dr O'Keeffe came straight away and summoned the ambulance from Skibbereen to take Mary to Cork General Hospital. He wrote a note for the cancer specialist, Dr Hurley, under whom Mary had been receiving treatment and she was away soon after nine am. I telephoned the hospital at about midday and was told that she was still in Out Patients and was advised to ring again at about three pm. This I did and was told that my darling wife was still down in Out Patients and had not yet been seen by Dr Hurley. I blew my top at this information and demanded to be put through to Dr Hurley. As luck would have it he was contacted on his walkie talkie and I was able to tell him what had happened. He was very concerned at what I told him and promised to look into the matter straight away. I telephoned again at four pm and learned, to my intense relief, that she had been admitted to hospital and was under the care of Dr Hurley. All this activity at South View, Leap had been observed by Dinny Carthy, our gardener who lived across the valley from us. He had observed the arrival of the ambulance and, as is the custom amongst the Irish country folk, he called during the morning to find out what had happened. Perhaps one has become cynical in one's dotage, but it is my belief that the Irish country folk have a morbid curiosity in what has befallen their neighbours. This is not to say that their sympathy is not entirely genuine but, like us all, they like to know what is happening and are not afraid to be seen to enquire.

The next day I went in to see her and she was on 'platelettes'. The Ward Sister told me that Mary was responding to treatment but that she was in isolation and that I had to wear a sterilized gown and mask if I wished to see her. This gave us something to laugh about! After about ten days she was discharged and

Margot Tucker came to visit us. Margot's sister had been a hospital matron so Margot arrived armed with an assortment of useful gadgets such as an alarm bell and a bed pan. After Margot's departure we kept going as best we could, making the most of each day as it came. Patrick and his wife, Cathy and Richard with his wife, Judith, came to visit us periodically and Mary was especially delighted to have a visit from her nephew Michael Harrison and his wife, Lis, just about a month before she died. Her brother Ted and sister-in-law Bee were frequent visitors but I regret we were not very sociable and we seemed to resent the intrusion of others. We were lucky in that there was a trained nurse in the village who called every morning to give Mary a wash and brush up and Dr O'Keeffe called each and every Monday after his visit to the village clinic to monitor her progress, and she had been bed-bound now for about a month. Another nurse, Maureen Crowley, who had also become a good friend took on night duty so I would get some sleep.

On Monday, 6 July, Dr O'Keeffe called as usual and found Mary in a very weak state. He called me to one side and said: 'You may start making your arrangements now.'

I knew immediately what he meant and that evening I telephoned my sons in the Isle of Man. Patrick arrived on 9 July, just in time to see and be recognized by his mother. Richard came a day later, on the afternoon of 10 July and his mother had passed away that morning. Ted Scott was able to tell me the name of the Undertakers in Bandon and he also arranged for the grave digger to prepare a spot for Mary in the churchyard at Rathclaren where she and I had been married just over thirty-one years previously. Mary was taken down to the little church in Leap where we had worshipped most Sundays and the funeral service took place on Monday, 13 July at Rathclaren, followed by tea at The Glen which was organized most efficiently by Bee. I do not think I could have coped with the trauma without the support of my in-laws at The Glen and, of course, my two sons who stayed with me until the 18 July. After their departure I do remember that I broke down and had a jolly good cry — and felt much better for it!

An air of unreality hung over me for many days after the sons returned to their own lives on the Isle of Man and I remember very little about it all. The district nurse called on me every Thursday afternoon and took tea with me, and Joan David from up the lane fussed over me like an old hen even though I would rather be left alone to cope with life on my own and in my own way. I would go over to The Glen for lunch on a Sunday and I was asked out to dinner parties on occasions. I remember once being asked out by 'Poogie' Richardson to dinner one evening when the Scotts and the Welplys were there. I was placed at the head of the table and I suddenly realized that I was being used — I was not asked for myself, I was useful for making up numbers.

Towards the end of August I decided to go away and proceeded to plan a great round of visits, starting with the Isle of Man, thence on to the Strettons in Cumbria, Kathleen Bibby at Beverley in East Yorkshire, the Grays in Baslow, the Beringers in Sussex, the Chicks in Gloucestershire and then home. I must have picked up some bug or other en route because after I had left the Strettons I did not feel at all well. I visited Richmond in North Yorkshire and found the place of my birth and thence went on to Beverley which was not a great success as I felt really off colour. Talking over old times with Kathleen did not help and I was forced to retire to bed. All I wanted was to return home so I rang the Grays to excuse myself and made a bee-line for home. This was a great pity as it would have been fun to talk over pre-war days in Sheffield with Kathleen who was, incidentally, the widow of Alan Bibby, the brother of Colin who had married Muriel, my half-aunt! Back home at last I found a tea tray all neatly laid out for me by Joan David whom I had told of my early return, and then I got down to the business of clearing up the paper work connected with Mary's death. Hugh Ludlow, our solicitor in Dunmanway, dealt with all the paper work connected with probate and he was like a father to me and I can never thank him enough for all his support at this time. All sorts of problems had to be sorted out and thanks to Hugh this work was accomplished with the minimum of hassle.

Come the Christmas I set off once more for the Isle of Man. On arrival I found myself in the midst of a family football match in which I was the football! Patrick and Cathy were moving from their bungalow to a farm at West Baldwin where Patrick had been appointed farm manager. I spent a few days with Richard and Judith at their home at Mount Pleasant, East Foxdale before being switched to Patrick's new home at West Baldwin for the actual Christmas Day festivities. Thence back to Mount Pleasant for the New Year where there was a party and so back home with a sigh of relief. During this time I received a letter from Viola Wilding of Rossana House, Ashford, County Wicklow where Richard had once been employed. She was spending her Christmas with her brother and sister-in-law at Newark. Neither of us was enjoying our Christmas much and we both agreed we would not do the same thing again. For my part I was missing Mary and just could not enter into the party spirit.

22

Vi came to stay with me over the Easter period 1982 and we also spent a long weekend together at Virginia after which I asked her to marry me. We seemed to get on well together with our mutual interests in farming and all things rural. Vi had been widowed since 1974 and we were married in Ross Cathedral by Peter Fleming on 14 July 1982, the day before Peter left Rosscarberry for his retirement near Fermoy; I was particularly anxious for Peter to marry us because I held him in high regard and also it was his half-brother who had married Mary and me way back in 1950.

Vi and I settled down to our new life together at Leap and I began to enjoy life and its vicissitudes once more. Vi had problems at Rossana, her old home, so these had to be attended to and we made frequent visits up to County Wicklow to try to sort things out. Her son and daughter-in-law were making life very difficult for her, and me, and I still believe to this day that they were terrified lest I should come in and spoil their plans to take over Rossana House and run it as a Guest House. They gave us the impression that they were anxious to have a settlement and as a consequence we made several visits and engaged Counsel to advise us, but all to no avail. It all cost us a great amount of money but at last the penny dropped — they did not intend doing a deal at all but rather to clean us out of all our means on lawyers' fees. Fortunately for us, we too had friends, and through the good offices of one of them, a neighbour offered to buy Vi's shares in the company. At the time of her husband's death in 1974 she had been badly advised by her solicitor and as a result she had handed over too many shares to her son, thus depriving herself of occupying the driver's seat. Apparently father and son did not get on well since the son had married a local girl of whom his parents disapproved and his father had left the bulk of his estate to his wife (Vi). The other party soon cottoned on to this dilemma and blocked her at every turn — so much so that when she was offered a million and a quarter pounds for her shares her son refused the offer and said he wanted a million and a half! I took an instant dislike to the daughter-in-law and had no intention whatsoever of moving into Rossana so, after much manoeuvring and backbiting, it was finally agreed that Vi would part with her shares and leave her son in sole possession. This left us free to get on with our own lives. We sold up at Leap and moved over to Cumbria, to a small medieval village called Milburn, in the Eden Valley, about eight miles from Penrith and about twelve miles from the Strettons who lived in a castle at Dacre.

It was now May 1985 when we arrived in Milburn and we were soon enveloped in village affairs. An invitation arrived from the Over Sixties Club inviting us to join them in their annual outing, a mystery tour which turned out to be a most enjoyable coach tour around the neighbourhood including the Yorkshire Moors, Sedburgh and environs, finishing up with a meal at the Royal Oak Inn at Appleby. It appeared that our arrival had caused some headaches amongst the committee members of the Over Sixties Club for they were not sure whether we qualified for inclusion in their outing! As I was just coming up to my sixty-fifth birthday I took that to be a compliment indeed!

As new arrivals we were asked to judge the Fancy Dress parade at the village fete but I was afflicted with back trouble and so we were let off. I was also detailed by Gwen Aynsley to open the annual village horticultural show in September which I did to the best of my ability and Patrick and Cathy came to stay with us over the Christmas period. Cathy was pregnant at the time so her activities were restricted. It snowed heavily but they were able to get away on time before further snow falls made life in the countryside somewhat difficult. It reminded me of winters in Sheffield and I liked it but Vi did not care much for the Cumbrian climate and she found the cold and damp weather gave her aches and pains.

Richard and Judith, together with Maria, came to spend some of their summer holiday with us in the May and they were followed by Guy and Nettie Beringer from Sussex who were on their way home from a holiday in Scotland. As the climate was not to Vi's liking we put the house in the hands of Messrs Gibbings and Thornborrow of Penrith and had several people to view it. We had spent a little money on the place, notably installing new Night Store heaters and also an automatic Gas cooker. We had also created a very attractive (we thought) garden to the rear by taking out a large, overgrown herbaceous flower bed and creating a rounded feature with a weeping Birch Tree in the middle. We laid concrete paths interspersed with gravel under which we put plastic sheeting to prevent the intrusion of unwanted weeds. The whole effect was most appealing as well as saving us a great deal of work!

The advertisement for the house stated a price guide of £46,000 although to give them their due, the Agents had suggested a figure nearer £50,000. I was anxious to sell and did not want to put off any potential buyers and anyway, the price of £46,000 was only a guide! Whilst all this was going on we had to decide where we were going to live and we finally decided on the Isle of Man because my two sons and their families were there and we did not particularly wish to return to Ireland at that time. An amusing incident occurred in this connection. On one of our visits to the island we were having a dinner party at the Tynwald Restaurant and considered it only right and proper that the young people should be aware of what was in our minds. I therefore said to the assembled company:

'Vi and I are thinking seriously of coming over to the island to live. What do you think and have you any objections?'

Immediately came a reply from Judith.

'You please yourselves. We have our own circle of friends!'

Suitably deflated and as no one else seemed to have any opinion, we let the matter drop.

We had been in touch with two Estate Agents on the island and had given them precise details of what we were looking for. We wanted a bungalow with three bedrooms, within easy walking distance of a shop for milk, bread and papers, and preferably a paddock but this was not a pre-requisite. All sorts of properties were offered to us and when we were over on a visit we called at Chrystals to expostulate. Their computer had, in fact, got all the details of what we wanted and when we had had our say we were told of Doway, Strang Road, in Union Mills on offer at £69,000. We went to see it and, whilst it had not got a paddock, the accommodation and situation were just what we wanted so back we went to the agent and put in our offer of £65,000. The young man who attended to us was Tony Knowles who was an Old Malvernian! We were told to return in the afternoon when he would have a reply for us and we finally settled on a figure of £66,500, to include all carpets and curtains. May Corlett, Patrick's mother-in-law asked us if we were sure we would fit in. She is a Lancashire lass and maybe she knew something or was she trying to tell us something? We would find out in due course.

We moved from Milburn to the Isle of Man on 5 August and caught the one am sailing from Heysham. We were entertained to dinner on the night of our departure by the Strettons at Dacre Castle and then we set off from there complete with a loaded trailer on the back of the car! The keys of the house were at the Central Stores, Union Mills which had been arranged with Richard so we were able to prepare for the arrival of our furniture which had come over with us per Messrs Pollard & Sons; theirs was the cheapest quote we could get! In the midst of the unloading, Ken Adams from the Central Stores, Union Mills turned up bearing a pot plant as a welcoming gift.

On the following Thursday we went to the Royal Agricultural Show at Sulby in the north of the island. It had been a wet summer and the entrance/exit to the show ground was a quagmire so we did not stay long. Shortly after our arrival on the island we saw an article in the local newspaper announcing the formation of an Action Group of Strang Road resident's under a Dr Peggy Pilsworth of Hy Holme, Strang Road to fight the proposed development of Camlork Farm lands which were situated just behind our property. We joined this group and, as an aside, we refused to pay the Advocate for his work as we had not been told of this proposal. After some delay the advocate, Mr John Crellin of Messrs T.W. Cain & Sons of Athol Street in Douglas, suggested taking off their extraneous expenses amounting to some £400 and we accepted his proposal. I suppose we should have held out for more — in fact it was suggested we could have sued the firm for neglecting to tell us about the development plan but, as we were English and not Manx, we did not feel we could win! I think Richard considers we were foolish not to have a go but we had spent too much time in Ireland, also a Celtic country, and could guess what would be the outcome!

We soon settled into our new home and the first callers were the Alstons who lived down the road at Cherry Tree Lodge. The land on which our bungalow was built used to be part of the garden of Cherry Tree Lodge in the days when that house was owned by Mr and Mrs Harris. Mr Harris was a well known figure in the island and we were told that Harris Promenade on the Douglas sea front was named after him. Anyway, after his death, his son came back from Australia, sold off the family home and built himself our bungalow and transferred the name from the old family house. The Alstons came with pot of chrysanthemums to welcome us and they were the only people to show any interest in us new arrivals. We got to know the Pilsworths because of the Action Group and, apart from these two families, we were left severely alone. The following spring whilst returning from lunch at the Sefton Hotel, we saw there was a dog show on at St Andrew's Church Hall at the end of Finch Road so we wandered in to see what was going on. There we made the acquaintance of Margaret Buttimore who lived over the wall from us and fronted on to Strang Road. She was showing her Chihuahuas (desert rats as I call them!) It transpired that her husband, Frank, who sported a thick beard, hailed from Garretstown in County Cork so we had something in common in that regard. Margaret had been a teacher before her marriage and they had three sons and a daughter. One son, Simon, was a wood carver — and an irritating noise he made too! He and the dogs were a constant source of annoyance to us but enquiries revealed that there is no law against noise in a residential area so we just had to grin and bear it. Our predecessors from whom we had purchased Doway did in fact mention that they had had to complain to a neighbour about a yapping dog nearby and I have often wondered since then whether the Buttimore's dogs were the culprits!

Since our first brush with the Department of the Environment we have had numerous skirmishes with the authorities including two public hearings under Deemster Luft at the Union Mills Methodist Hall. Peggy Pilsworth was the leading light in the resistance to the proposed development and since her untimely death the leadership has been taken over by John Kermode with myself acting as public relations and press officer. It would be a crying shame if the authorities were allowed to get away with it. Chris Simpson of Mill Baldwin Ltd is the leading light for the opposition — his building company has purchased some ten acres of the farm lands with an option to purchase a further fifty acres for development. I have heard that Simpson is quite certain that he will eventually win. Maybe he will but it has been great fun opposing him! So far we have managed to hold him off for five years and we are all prepared to do battle again if the need arises! We discovered, too, that the Alstons were somewhat piqued at our buying Doway because they wanted it themselves but were away in Scotland when Mr Wheeler put the place on the market. So they came back home to find that it had been sold. There is a Right of Way along the bottom of the garden leading from our driveway entrance to his land next door. He also has a Right of Way up our avenue and every time he comes to visit us he makes a point of reminding us of these facts!

It was not long before we began to realize what was behind May Collect's remark about fitting in. This is a funny country; a real mixed bag of folk all mixed up together and there seem to be very few people like us. They are twitchy and easily take offence and one has to choose ones words carefully to avoid causing animosity. Vi finds it very difficult socially but so far I have managed to cope. The difference here being the fact that I have had to muck in and rub shoulders with all sorts of different types both during my war service and also during my time in business. Vi, on the other hand, started at a disadvantage in this respect. Her family did not mix with the villagers and took up farming so she did not mix much with the hoi polloi! We have both of us agreed that we do not particularly want to turn our toes up in this country — but the puzzle is where to go. We hanker after the Irish Republic in many ways and feel that maybe we should have joined Esmé McDonagh at Clonmannon, but it is rather too near Rossana! Should we go back to England? If so, where to? My own Sheffield roots have dried up after nearly twenty-five years away and Vi's relations have all passed on except for Mary Harrison (Mary Mac) in Gainford. My two sons over here with their families, do not really want us and anyway they are becoming more Manx than the Manx themselves if that is possible! The politics stinks — out of a population of about 70,000 the persons in charge of departments call themselves Ministers and even in Ireland some would be hard put to get a seat on a County Council! Enquiries of a reputable Estate Agent last year revealed that our bungalow was worth £175,000. The other day (November 1990) the same agents quoted us a figure of £220,000!

In March 1990 we decided that we would have our autumn break in the UK and I felt constrained to do a sentimental tour round my childhood haunts. Accordingly we booked ourselves into the Fossebridge Inn in Gloucestershire, the Metropole Hotel in Llandrindod Wells (in Wilding Country) and the Whitwell Hall Country House Hotel near York. We had seen an article in the *Daily Telegraph* some years ago in which the latter hostelry was written about in glowing terms. We were told that it was run by a retired Lieutenant Commander and that there were to be no children under the age of twelve years. I had cut this article out for future reference and now seemed as good a time as any to stay there and at the same time make the acquaintance of Mr and Mrs Humphrey Moore who lived near York and who had written a book on the Davy family. I had been in correspondence with them and now was the chance to meet them personally. His mother was a Davy and he (Humphrey) was interested in Genealogy as a hobby. I felt it would be nice and satisfying to fit a face to the name.

We booked ourselves in to both the Fossebridge Inn and the Whitwell Hall Hotel on a Bed and Breakfast basis — and weren't we fortunate! The price tag at Fossebridge was sixty-three pounds for a twin room with breakfast and the Whitwell Hall was sixty-five pounds. The latter's price, although somewhat steep, did not unduly disturb me as I felt it would probably be worthwhile to be free of small children who can be a real nuisance in a hotel, particularly in these days when very few parents seem to exercise any control over their young. We were far from satisfied with the first stop. On presenting ourselves for dinner on the first night we were dismayed to find the menu was the same à la carte menu each night. It was pretty obvious that the food came out of the deep freeze and was not very tempting. Our bill for the first night's dinner was £37 pounds plus a further £8.50 for a bottle of wine, making a total of £45.50 for a somewhat indifferent meal. The following night we went into the bar. Again exactly the same menu but the prices were very different. Our bill read: 2 x Soup £5.00, 1 x Marie Rose Prawns £4.95 and 1 x Red Mullet £7.95. Total £17.90. Quite a difference to the dining room bill! After that we decided that it would be better value at the Little Chef restaurant which we had spotted near Northleach so thither we went for the ensuing three nights and enjoyed fish and chips with a cup of tea for under £10 for the two of us! The surroundings may not have been all that salubrious and I do not consider myself miserly but I do like value for my money. I had enquired from the proprietor of the Inn as to who lived at the Mill House and was informed that the present owners were Lord and Lady Banbury. I took Vi down to see my old home where we lived when I was between the ages of about six and ten years but the hedges had grown high and it was impossible to see the house from the other side of the river. We did call there before our departure and were met by the Spanish butler-cum-handyman who was kind enough to show us round. Lord and Lady Banbury were away and had left their baby in the charge of nanny, and the Spanish houseman and his wife were left in charge of the property. The former was obviously very proud of all he had done and I must say we were most impressed too. The river had been drained and he had built retaining walls along the banks. There was now a hard tennis court and a swimming pool and the gardens had been extended to incorporate much that had been waste land when we had lived there. There was no flooding now that the river had been cleared of weed and retaining walls had been built. Altogether a very desirable residence and was a perfect example of what can be done when the owners have a bit of brass to spare. Not a very easy place to re-sell I imagine but in these days of easy money, who cares?

From Fossebridge we travelled on to Llandrindod Wells in Powys, Central Wales so that Vi could visit her first husband's grave and those of his family. She was also anxious to show me the Elan Valley where five reservoirs had been created to provide a water supply for the city of Birmingham. On arrival we were immediately struck by the warmth of the welcome at the Hotel

Metropole where we had booked in under the title of Country Retreat at £85.00 for a twin bedded room with dinner, bed and breakfast. The staff were efficient and cheerful and we considered it to be jolly good value and I was compelled to revise my opinion of the Welsh! We were somewhat dismayed to find there was little if any reference to the Wilding family who had, in fact, founded the hotel — then known as the Bridge Hotel in Coaching Days — some 200 years ago. There was a large portrait painting of a Mrs Miles in the foyer and she was designated as 'Our Founder'. We went up to the Golf Club which Vi's father-in-law had laid out, on Wilding Land, and were both surprised and disgusted to find absolutely no reference to the Wildings at all.

On our return home I made a point of writing to my step son-in-law to tell him about our visit and about the fact that the Wildings seemed to have been forgotten. Whilst in the district we had 'pub grub' at the Severn Arms Hotel at Penybont. This used to be another Wilding establishment and the landlord and his wife, Mr and Mrs Lloyd were much more clued up on the family associations. Some of the female family members had married in the district so that the family connections were still kept alive there.

We then moved on to Yorkshire for our three nights at the Whitwell Hall Country House Hotel. On arrival there we were met at the front door by the Proprietor who greeted us with outstretched hand and the information that he was Lieutenant Commander Peter Milner. I replied that if we are to exchange ranks then I was Major Davy, late of the Indian Army!

We were allotted a room on the second (or servant's) floor which entailed ascending a second flight of stairs approached through a swing door leading off the main gallery. We were more than 'put out' by this development particularly as we had booked in the month of March, six months beforehand. An ancient retainer gave us a hand up with our suitcases. The room itself was quite comfortable and was equipped with all the necessities that one has come to expect these days such as tea and coffee making facilities, telephone, electric alarm-cum-clock and, of course, the en suite facilities. I imagine this was once the housekeeper's room or maybe the butler's! It was adjacent to the staff quarters and there was a creaking floor board outside our door which used to waken us at about midnight. We soon discovered that the bar staff did not know how to serve Ginger Wine or a Gin and Mixed so we settled for an Orange Squash and a Gin and Tonic! The dinner menu consisted of four courses, inclusive of coffee, and was priced at £19.50 per person! I thought this was rather too much so we only ate there once and subsequently repaired to the nearest Little Chef for the customary fish and chips plus a cup of tea for under £10 for the two of us!

In the dining room was a huge centre table laid up with about twenty places with silver candelabras containing candles all lit up. We awaited in eager anticipation the entry of those for whom this high table was laid but as no one of undue importance appeared, we assumed that this was only for show. Subsequent enquiries confirmed our surmise. The centre table was always laid up and the candles lighted to add dignity to the proceedings — for the benefit of any American guests no doubt!

EPILOGUE

The date is 1 September 1990. I have completed my allotted span according to the Scriptures, but I may be so strong as to complete a further ten years, thus fulfilling the promise that man may be so strong as to complete four score years, I do hope so as I find life to be so interesting and exciting.

Now to fill in the gaps -

I have not mentioned the time when my father told me to go back and return the apples which I had taken from Mr Rodger's tree. Not far distant from our home there lived a farmer named Rodgers whose yard and garden were surrounded by a high brick wall. There was an apple tree growing the other side of the wall, whose branches, laden with red and succulent fruit, hung across the wall and I was just able to reach them by standing on the cross-bar of my bicycle. On his finding out about this misdemeanour on my part, my father sent me back to return the apples and to be sure that I apologized to either Mr or Mrs Rodgers 'Thou shalt not steal'.

I have not mentioned the time when, in class at Dorchester, one of my pupils told me I was on fire. The class had done a particularly bad French prep (or homework). I was enjoying a pipeful of tobacco during break when the bell sounded for the start of the next lesson. I put the lighted pipe in my jacket pocket before entering the class room and proceeded to admonish the children about the appalling standard of their homework. A pupil at the back of the class shouted out:

'Sir, you're on fire!'

'Don't be impertinent,' I replied.

Then I discovered smoke pouring from my jacket pocket. My lighted pipe had ignited the lining of my pocket!

I have not mentioned the time when Mary and I were staying

196

with the Beringers near Haywards Heath in the year 1975. I had cause to go up to London on business and Guy Beringer told me to be careful, on my return, to take the through train from Waterloo to Brighton which only stopped at Haywards Heath, otherwise the journey would take too long. On presenting my Return ticket at the barrier to the West Indian ticket inspector on duty, I enquired of him from which platform the Brighton train departed.

'It's on the board,' he replied.

There are or were some fifteen platforms and I couldn't see the information I required. As I was patrolling the platforms I was accosted by an Indian lady, dressed in a sari, who said,

'Excuse me, but are you wanting the Brighton train?'

On my saying that I did so want that train she told me that it left from number twelve platform. She knew because she did that journey frequently and was catching it that day. I have often wondered since whether I would have the nerve to tell an Indian such information if I were in Calcutta or Delhi. Probably not!

Early on in my business career in Sheffield I had a permanent booking at the City Hall to hear the fortnightly concert of the Halle Orchestra under the baton of Sir John Barbirolli. In the seat next to me, also with a season ticket, was a gentleman with whom I got into conversation. He was a coal miner from Barnsley and we became very friendly as we both enjoyed the music and were great admirers of Sir John Barbirolli. His name was Fred though I never discovered his surname.

We have been fascinated by the assortment of motor cycles which arrive on the island from across the water for each and every T.T. Some of these machines are really super and can cost about £10,000 to £12,000. Personally I would rather have a hood over me for that sort of money! Underneath their crash helmets and leathers they are mostly very agreeable people and their whole uniform belies them! There is a virtual take-over of the island when the T.T. and the subsequent Grand Prix is on. The road outside our entrance is a mass of cars and bikes as Union Mills is a good vantage point where competitors go through the village at at least 100 miles per hour. The early morning practices which start at about six am are, admittedly, a trifle disturbing but we get used to that.

Vi's friend, Mary Harrison, came to stay with us in 1986 and we took her to the Gaiety Theatre in Douglas. She was quite charmed with the place which is, in fact, something unique in these days of mediocrity. The theatre was designed and built by Robert Macham in 1890 and is now, so I am told, the only one of its generation which has been retained entirely intact. The present manager, Mervin Stokes, is dedicated to its preservation and, indeed, to its restoration to its former Victorian grandeur and this year, the year of its hundredth anniversary, the Friends of the Gaiety of which we are members have resolved to raise enough monies to restore the theatre to its former glory. Mervin is obviously dedicated to his job as theatre manager but one cannot help but wonder how much encouragement he receives from the politicians who are very good at accepting the praise and getting the kudos but are even more adept at dodging the brickbats!

To be continued — D.V.!